LIFE TO THE FULL

Life to the Full

True Stories on the Dignity of Every Human Life

Edited by
Abby Johnson and Tyler Rowley

IGNATIUS PRESS SAN FRANCISCO

The stories in *Life to the Full* are personal testimonials, each relying on the author's memory. Errors in historical fact are not the responsibility of the publisher.

Cover photo ©iStock

Cover design by Kyle Rowley

ISBN 978-1-62164-454-5 (PB)
ISBN 978-1-64229-239-8 (eBook)
Library of Congress Control Number 2022950502
Printed in the United States of America ♾

To Saint Patrick

CONTENTS

FOREWORD

Dr. Meg Meeker

As a former pro-choice advocate and Gloria Steinem groupie, I understand a woman's rationale for having an abortion. A child not only interferes with her life plans, but forces a woman to stay connected to a man she never wants to see again. Women should always have control over what happens to them. At least, those were my sentiments until two things happened that turned my beliefs about abortion 180 degrees.

When I was practicing pediatrics as a young doctor, a sixteen-year-old girl came to my office in a panic. She was bleeding profusely. I examined her and learned that she had had an abortion twenty-four hours earlier. She was sobbing and in excruciating pain. I knew I needed to get her to an ob-gyn. I tried to call the doctor who did the abortion. He wouldn't speak to me. Admitting to a complication from his "surgical procedure" would be a liability. I then called an ob-gyn who I knew didn't perform abortions. He wouldn't see the little girl either because he didn't want to "mop up someone else's mess". Again, liability isn't something anyone wants to take on.

But there was more. Her abortion hadn't been "complete". She had residual fetal tissue that could cause life-threatening problems. Suddenly, abortion became a reality to me. It wasn't an idea, belief, or philosophy. Women were cut, and babies were torn apart. Young girls had contractions so severe that they thought they would pass out. They got infections, depression, and post-traumatic stress disorder, and I wasn't equipped to deal with these because, after all, I was taught that abortions done in a safe environment were straightforward and without many complications. For the first time in my medical career, I saw a beautiful young patient I wasn't equipped to help. And sadly, I had a difficult time finding a physician who *was* equipped. Seeing a patient with such a life-threatening problem was disturbing to the core, and I felt sick to my stomach. Clearly, I saw that abortion was no easy option for anyone—young girls, women, physicians, or other medical workers, no matter what anyone says.

Life to the Full is a chilling but critical compilation of true stories about the struggles women, girls, and physicians confront with abortion. Compared to the memoirs in this book, my own seems like light reading. The dramatic testimonies that Tyler and Abby have collected teach us what women and men really go through during pregnancy and abortion. The stories are exactly what every one of us, on both sides of the abortion issue, need to hear, because they are a reality. They are about real people with real experiences. They are hard to read; they might make you cry. But that's exactly what we need to do: mourn; for it is only in mourning that we can be moved deeply enough to fight to make a difference. The fight for a right to life is a grueling one because it is more than a disagreement: it is a war. Human lives are at stake. Beliefs must be upended and worldviews changed. Some will feel guilty and others ashamed. We don't want to proselytize or impose our own religious convictions, and yet when we stand and speak out for the unborn and young women carrying them, we cannot help but address the meaning of life itself.

Abby and Tyler bring us to a point where we must make a choice: either move forward into the fight or run like cowards. They make us uncomfortable with ourselves, and this is a good thing. Good things never come about when comfort abounds. After reading *Life to the Full*, you will feel uncomfortable, and this is exactly what, I believe, God wants. We will never save babies, women, and young girls from the horrors of abortion until we are ready to allow ourselves to live with profound uneasiness and to grieve deeply.

PREFACE

Tyler Rowley

> The day that people lose their horror for abortion will be the most terrible day for humanity.
>
> —Saint Padre Pio

"I know the abortion issue as perhaps no one else does. . . . I helped nurture the creature in its infancy by feeding it great draughts of blood and money." These are the words of Bernard Nathanson, founder of the National Association for the Repeal of Abortion Laws (NARAL), and appropriately nicknamed "the Grandfather" of the abortion industry. During the 1970s, he ran the largest abortion operation in the United States, and as its director oversaw seventy-five thousand abortions.

As a child, Nathanson witnessed his father's incessant psychological abuse of his mother and mocking of belief in God at every opportunity. At nineteen, after learning his girlfriend was pregnant, Nathanson sought his father's counsel. His father, a doctor himself, responded by mailing him five hundred dollars for an abortion.

The corrupt witness of an evil and abusive father led the young Nathanson not just to atheism, but to a career in killing. From 1973 to 1980, Nathanson personally killed thousands of unborn children, including two of his own.

Then, on the feast of the Immaculate Conception in 1996, at Saint Patrick's Cathedral in New York City, Bernard

Daniel Nathanson was baptized, confirmed, and received the Body and Blood of Jesus Christ.

In a quiet chapel below the main altar, one of the world's most compelling stories—not unlike some passages of the New Testament—reached its conclusion: the founder of NARAL had repented, discovered the love and mercy of God, converted to Christ, and dedicated himself to pro-life activism. He would spend the rest of his life making amends for his sins.

Preceding the conferral of the sacraments, Cardinal John O'Connor remarked in his homily that the lack of respect for life is rooted in a lack of self-respect, and that a lack of self-respect is a consequence of sin. How fitting it was, the Cardinal continued, that Dr. Nathanson should enter the Church on the feast of Mary's Immaculate Conception, by which God, our true Father, untied the knot of sin for mankind.

Influenced by philosophy, scientific discovery, and powerful ultrasound technology, Nathanson had adopted his pro-life position around 1980. Nine more years passed before he surrendered to belief in God.

What was the impetus for this avowed atheist's conversion? Surely it was a gradual process, or as Nathanson put it: "I went through a ten-year transitional time . . . when I felt the burden of sin growing heavier and more insistent." Nathanson recounts a cold January morning at Planned Parenthood on Manhattan's Lower East Side when he joined 1,200 other pro-lifers with their arms wrapped around one another, singing hymns while blocking the entrance to the killing center. "It was only then," he later wrote, "that I apprehended the exaltation, the pure love on the faces of that shivering mass of people."

He listened as they prayed.

> They prayed, they supported and encouraged each other, they sang hymns of joy, and they constantly reminded each other of the absolute prohibition against violence. It was, I suppose, the sheer intensity of the love that astonished me: They prayed for the unborn babies, for the confused and frightened pregnant women, and for the doctors and nurses in the clinic. They even prayed for the police and the media who were covering the event. They prayed for each other, but never for themselves. And I wondered: How can these people give of themselves for a constituency that is (and always will be) mute, invisible, and unable to thank them? . . . I was shaken by the intensity of the spirituality at these demonstrations. . . . Even the police hung back, in deference, I believe, to the purity of the action. . . . It was not until I saw the spirit put to the test on those bitterly cold demonstration mornings, with pro-choicers hurling the most fulsome epithets at them, the police surrounding them, the media openly unsympathetic to their cause, the federal judiciary fining and jailing them, and municipal officials threatening them—all through it they sat smiling, quietly praying, singing, confident and righteous of their cause and ineradicably persuaded of their ultimate triumph.[1]

"It was then," he added, "that I began seriously to question what indescribable force generated them to this activity. Why, too, was I there? What had led me to this time and place? Was it the same Force that allowed them to sit serene and unafraid at the epicenter of legal, physical, ethical, and moral chaos? And for the first time in my entire adult life, I began to entertain seriously the notion of God."[2]

[1] Bernard Nathanson, *The Hand of God: A Journey from Death to Life by the Abortion Doctor Who Changed His Mind* (Washington, D.C.: Regnery, 2013), 193.

[2] Nathanson, *The Hand of God*, 193.

Sometimes, it seems, the truth just can't be grasped until one directly encounters it. For Nathanson to become pro-life, he needed to encounter a child's image on an ultrasound machine. For him to become Catholic, he needed to encounter the love of Christians.

Nathanson's dramatic conversion was an encounter with Christ, who led him to abandon a former way of life. Jesus taught in various ways: by asking questions, making direct statements, quoting Scripture, using metaphors, and especially by telling stories. Stories are powerful, creating bridges from abstract ideas to concrete reality. Stories serve to inject ideas into the imagination, illustrating what mankind can and should be. The stories Jesus told illuminate the deepest truths of how God works. In fact, the Scriptures are filled with stories. While often messy and strange, they always point to the core message that God loves us and wants us to live *life to the full.*

Jesus Himself is the personification of God's story—the mind of God come to life. And through the life of Christ, God speaks to us in a language we can best understand: *a life fully lived.* A perfect life, played out on Earth's stage, with the script recorded so we can play it over and over again. Jesus reveals the life of God to us in the greatest story God could tell His children.

Pontius Pilate entered into this story by asking, "What is truth?" and in so doing gave voice to the question that nestles in the souls of all men. Often, however, we miss the plain truth right before our eyes because we are busy conforming the truth to ourselves, instead of conforming ourselves to the truth.

Worthy tales offer a solution to our lack of prudence and wisdom, spotlighting truths that can be transported across cultures and over centuries, ultimately penetrating our stubborn egos. They serve to instruct and inspire, taking the hearer on a journey from one perspective to another, or, from abstraction to incarnation. And because of that, they're memorable. It is said that people are twenty-two times more likely to remember a story than a fact.

One of the most important tools in the abortion fight is the ultrasound. Why? Because it conveys a story, however brief, of a child's life. Just one blip of a heartbeat—one glimpse of the body on the screen—and it's suddenly impossible to avoid an encounter with the truth. One can try to conjure up all of the arguments for why abortion should be legal, and all the reasons why reality must bend to the will, but they lie impotent against the story of that tiny body and the thumping of that heart.

Pregnancy centers across the country report that most abortion-minded women choose life for their child after seeing or hearing an ultrasound. Perhaps understandably, a woman might initially think of the baby in her womb in a remote, objective way. But the ultrasound whispers to her the remarkable story of *her* child, a story that cuts to her heart and sticks in her mind. It was ultrasound technology that prompted Nathanson to abandon the abortion movement. He called the innovative technology "the window into the womb."[3]

I return to our Lord again: one could think of Jesus as the ultrasound of God. "He is the image of the invisible God," as Saint Paul tells us (Col 1:15). Like the ultrasound of an unborn baby, when you see Him, you cave to the transcendent, because He reveals the joyous truth you know in your

[3] Nathanson, *The Hand of God*, 125.

heart—no matter how hard you may have tried to ignore it—that life is meaningful, much bigger than yourself, and governed by love.

Stories. Truth. Love. This is how you convert people—to the pro-life cause, as well as to Christ. In the pages of this book, you will find real-life stories expressed in authentic, self-giving love that tell the truth about abortion and show the dignity of every person. The goal of this book is to accomplish what hundreds of hours of lectures on embryology simply cannot: to convict every person that abortion is never the right choice. *Never.*

Someone once asked me what type of story I would want my children to write of me someday. What an interesting, if not intimidating, question. It made me realize that every child will ultimately craft a narrative of his parents, even if it exists only in his mind. A child possesses intimate details and profound impressions of how his mother and father raised him. Powerful memories. Lessons received. Virtues nurtured. Vices inherited. Every child has a story of his mom and dad. It is well attested that Saint Padre Pio could read the souls of his penitents in the confessional. A woman once came to him and confessed a dream that she would experience repeatedly, a simple dream of a man dressed in white, standing on a hill. She asked him what the meaning of the dream could be.

"It's your son, whom you aborted. He was going to be the pope."

Every *aborted* child has a story of his mom and dad.

On December 14, 2012, President Barack Obama addressed the nation with these words about children who perished before their rightful time: "They had their entire lives ahead of them—birthdays, graduations, weddings, kids of their own." Here, Obama is lamenting the loss of innocent children at the hands of a gunman in a speech concerning gun rights. But his words echo loudly the message pro-lifers have been repeating for fifty years: we are aborting our future; we are killing innocent children with full lives ahead of them!

For some reason, however, there exists an intellectual disconnect for people like President Obama when it comes to children inside and outside the womb. In a separate moment, Obama would inform a different audience that, if either of his two daughters ever "made a mistake," he wouldn't want them "punished with a baby," as he advocated for abortion rights.

Abortion is sixty-three million stories that were never told. Thousands of American classrooms of children wiped out and discarded as medical waste before they could experience the world and carve out their own lives. Abortion is sixty-three million stories, fashioned by the Author of Life, that never got past the first page. Lives that never felt the joy of birthdays, graduations, weddings, kids of their own.

The story of our Lord Jesus' incarnation began with Him as a miniscule unborn child in the womb of His Mother. God became a man, but He first became an embryo. That is why Christians get so frustrated with self-professed believers who identify themselves as pro-choice. A pagan is free to believe whatever he wants about the world, but it is simply impossible, once you attain faith in Christ, to miss the integral teaching that life in the womb must be loved. Christians believe that God became an unborn child—a fact that made an unborn John the Baptist leap for joy while still in the womb. This God grew within an immaculately conceived virgin-mother whose pregnancy led her to "magnify" God in her soul (see Lk 2). It is simply undeniable: love and dignity for unborn babies is built into the heart of the Church.

On March 25 the Catholic Church celebrates and contemplates the Annunciation, that moment when God sent an angel to announce the incomprehensible plan of salvation which would begin in the womb of a woman. It was intentional that Pope Saint John Paul II released on that date in 1995 a document called *Evangelium Vitae* (The Gospel of Life), in which, in no uncertain terms, he professes that abortion is always wrong. Listen to the first sentence of that document: "The gospel of life is at the heart of Jesus' message."[4] That is, the inherent worth of the human person, from the very first moment of his existence, is central to what the incarnate God tells us about Himself, His people, and His world. And then the next sentence: "It is to be preached with dauntless fidelity as good news to the people of every age and culture."[5]

Saint Patrick, Ireland's patron saint, was captured by pagan pirates as a teenager and sold into slavery in Ireland. He escaped several years later and returned to Britain, where he had a powerful vision of the children of Ireland reaching out their arms to him in desperation. It was this vision that made Patrick determined to return to Ireland and convert the pagan land to Christ. He faithfully undertook that mission and persevered through many hardships. Today, we find ourselves in a position similar to Saint Patrick's: surrounded by nonbelievers, facing criticism and opposition, with children desperately relying on us to rescue them.

It is our hope that the stories in this book will be an extension of our Lord's life, received by people of every age and culture as inspiration to put on the armor of God and fight for the millions of children reaching out to us from the womb, so that they may have life, and have it to the full.

[4] Pope John Paul II, *Evangelium Vitae* (Boston: Saint Paul Books and Media, 1995), 1.

[5] Pope John Paul II, *Evangelium Vitae*, 1.

INTRODUCTION

Abby Johnson

I met Erica many years ago and knew she was special almost immediately. A young mother of one son, she was pregnant again, and both she and her husband were thrilled. But early in the second trimester, she received a devastating personal diagnosis: stage IV inflammatory breast cancer. It had spread to her bones, and she was told that immediate treatment was the only chance to save her life. To her doctors, the life of her unborn baby was a hindrance, an obstacle to proper care. Despite tremendous pressure to abort her baby, Erica valiantly refused.

Erica's story inspired everyone, from her own supportive family and friends to her doctors, nurses, and caretakers. There was not one person who came into contact with Erica who was not somehow touched by the selfless and loving decision she made to carry her daughter, Ella, to term. *No one.*

All the stories in this book—including Erica's—reveal that choosing life is always the right choice, even in the midst of the most difficult circumstances. These are stories of hope, perseverance, and love—the kind of love that is selfless, giving, and sacrificial.

These stories are rarely told outside the intimate circles of families and friends, and yet they exist all around us in numbers known only to God. Moreover, the stories in this book represent the masses of people who have been hurt by abortion, and who have come to realize the tremendous gift that is life.

Sharing such stories sheds hope and light in this dark and desperate world. I hope this book is that consolation for you as it showcases the mercy of God through brave men and women who set aside their own lives for the lives of their children. We need these kinds of heroes today.

When Tyler Rowley approached me about compiling this book, I agreed wholeheartedly that sharing powerful stories about the value of life would touch hearts in a singular way. We needed to publish a book that convinces people abortion is *always* wrong in *every* circumstance, and that life is always the right choice. The best way to do that, we agreed, was to unleash some of the most powerful stories of lives that were changed by extraordinary grace. These stories will bring you to tears. I know they did for me, from the parents who sought the intercession of Father Michael McGivney, founder of the Knights of Columbus, for their unborn son who was given a death sentence in the womb, to the hospice nurse who was tapped to care for a disabled three-month-old baby and saw the awe-inspiring faith and love of his parents. And then there is singer and actress Joy Villa, who helps to lighten the mood with her trademark firecracker personality and heroic story of becoming a birthmother.

Today's culture is crying out for the hope these stories offer. Most people deeply want to hang on to something solid and strong and immovable in this life, but they often just don't know where to turn. Our culture has so twisted the word love that we cannot grasp its responsibilities—or its relationship to the unborn child.

This book shines light on real freedom and authentic love, which together require sacrifice, forgiveness, and occasional leaps of faith. This is the kind of love that Pope Saint John

Paul II always talked about, the love that is a self-gift, the love that often hurts, the love that is rooted in faith in Christ and never treats another human being as a means to an end.

Gaudium et Spes, one of the key documents of the Catholic Church's Second Vatican Council, states that "Man is the only creature on earth which God willed for itself, [and he] cannot fully find himself except through a sincere gift of himself." True love is almost always hard. But God has placed each of us on His heart as unique and unrepeatable individuals, and He asks us to imitate Him—even when it leads to the Cross.

Do children limit one's freedom? It depends on what you think freedom means. Does it mean staying out late at bars, sleeping in on weekends, not remembering what you did the night before? Freedom, better understood, means the forgiveness of our sins and being freed from the bonds of all those terrible inclinations to choose wrongly. When true freedom is accepted, instead of seeing a baby as an inconvenience, he becomes your joy. Watching a newborn sleep, hearing those precious first words, witnessing a toddler's first steps, and seeing little ones grow into loving boys and girls themselves—that's the joy of authentic freedom washing over your life.

Sometimes we are so deep in our sins that we don't even realize we are chained to them, and our freedom to love has been deeply compromised. I've had two abortions and now I have eight beautiful children. I can tell you I feel much freer being with my kids than living with the regret and pain of those past abortions. Many of us in the abortion industry would cope with our difficult jobs through alcohol, dark humor, and a variety of addictions. We needed to dull the pain of abortion, of being chained to that terrible evil. Working at an abortion clinic was a terrible ordeal.

But the worst part of it was working in the recovery room, where women who had just had abortions would be given juice and crackers before seeing themselves out the door. No one would talk but nearly everyone would be crying, some silently, others wailing out loud. Many former abortion workers say it was what they saw specifically in the recovery room that led them to quit the industry. It was a desolate and lonely place where most of the women who procured their abortions realized just how big of a mistake they had made. These women were chained to sin, so far from the freedom they truly desired. How they needed real and lasting love.

Yet, as I witnessed firsthand, through the grace of God, beauty can arise from those ashes. The more profound the sin, the more profound God's mercy. Although I repented of my grievous mistakes and saw the value of life, nothing prepared me for the kind of freedom that would come once I finally quit my job at Planned Parenthood.

I worked at Planned Parenthood in Bryan, Texas, for eight years, first as a volunteer and eventually as the director. I had a near-immediate conversion when I was called into the procedure room to hold an ultrasound probe over a young woman's abdomen so the abortion doctor could see exactly what he was doing. This kind of ultrasound-guided abortion wasn't necessarily unusual, but it wasn't typically done at my clinic. As I assisted the doctor and saw the thirteen-week-old unborn child being torn apart by the abortion instruments, something inside me broke. Questions bubbled up immediately: How did I not know this? How did I not know that life existed so obviously in the womb? I walked out of the clinic a week later and never looked back. Now that was true freedom.

I could almost feel the chains being broken when I walked

into the doors of the Coalition for Life, which had providentially established itself next door to the abortion clinic where I worked.

"But, Abby, come on, you've never had to live through the conception of a baby through rape or you've never had to deal with a devastating prenatal diagnosis. You have no idea of what you're talking about."

Even though I have not faced every situation of a woman in a crisis pregnancy, I've walked side by side with women who have. I have sat with them in their mess, prayed with them, provided financial assistance, and offered opportunities for healing. Moreover, our ministry, And Then There Were None, hosts healing retreats for former workers at abortion clinics (many of whom are post-abortive themselves) who have come face to face with the atrocities they participated in. When they share their stories and hear other women's stories, they transform right before our eyes. We can see their shoulders and facial muscles relax, their hands unclench, and the breath they were holding release as the weight of their burdens is lifted. It is truly incredible to see God's grace and mercy at work.

Every story in this book is unique, but the same thread of truth runs through each of them: that every life is valuable, that life exists in the womb, and that abortion is never the answer. Even in the most trying of circumstances—the single mother, the woman who was raped, the mother in jail, the woman in an abusive relationship, the parents given a heartbreaking diagnosis—abortion is always wrong. Every time. It is never the right decision to end innocent life in the womb, and if you're thinking of a particular situation that could be an exception, you may very well read about it in this book and change your mind.

While this book was being finalized, the U.S. Supreme

Court overturned the *Roe v. Wade* decision that legalized abortion through all nine months of pregnancy for any reason. The effect of the June 2022 Supreme Court ruling is that abortion rights will be decided by the individual states. So while we have taken a step forward as a nation, a great deal of work remains to be done.

God placed each one of these stories in this book for "such a time as this" (Esther 4:14) and for reasons that may be known only to Him.

I am praying for the day when abortion is unthinkable. May the stories in this book reach the hearts of men and women across this world until that petition is answered by our ever-patient God.

Ryan Tremblay

> Love is patient and kind; love is not jealous or boastful; it is not arrogant or rude. Love does not insist on its own way; it is not irritable or resentful; it does not rejoice at wrong, but rejoices in the right. Love bears all things, believes all things, hopes all things, endures all things. . . . So faith, hope, love abide, these three; but the greatest of these is love.
>
> —1 Corinthians 13:4–7, 13

These words of Saint Paul remain just that—words—until someone embodies them and turns them into spirit and life. The person in my life who made me see the true meaning of Saint Paul's words is my sister, Erica.

On the afternoon of Tuesday, June 23, 2015, I walked into Erica's hospital room with my guitar and asked her if she wanted me to sing a song for her. When I realized she couldn't respond due to her condition, I decided to play and sing her favorite song, "Amazing Grace (My Chains Are Gone)". When I finished singing the last word, Erica

---

Ryan Tremblay is a Catholic singer-songwriter, speaker, evangelist, and Educator. He has been featured on EWTN, CatholicTV, and Relevant Radio, and he has performed at World Youth Days in Poland and Panama. Ryan's latest album is entitled *TRUST: An EP for Erica*. He resides in Nashville, Tennessee with his beautiful wife, Elizabeth, and their triplet sons, and he serves Holy Rosary Academy in Nashville, Tennessee as both a performing artist and educator. For more information, music, and booking inquiries, visit RyanTremblayMusic.com.

opened her eyes and mouth as if she were going to speak. We sat up with excitement because it was a sign of hope. Seconds later, Erica took her last breath and was called home.

This is the story of Erica and a baby named Ella.

My sister was always an inspiration to me. As an older sibling, she influenced many aspects of my life, including my musical taste. She introduced me to the beautiful music of many Christian artists and encouraged me in my own musical pursuits. She always believed in me and supported me in my dream of spreading the good news through song. My entire musical career is owed to my big sister. Some people are born to inspire because their hearts are full of that greatest virtue.

When Erica was in ninth grade, she decided to raise money for children who were affected by HIV/AIDS, and she chose to donate the funds to Camp Heartland in Minnesota. Erica began her mission by placing coffee cans in every school in our hometown of Coventry, Rhode Island. The students were asked to put pennies into these cans and the donations quickly accumulated. Erica also coordinated a basketball game between the local high school faculty members and the police department. I remember when she called every "DeCosta" in the phone book until she reached the home of Sara DeCosta, the local Rhode Island sports legend and Olympic hockey gold medalist, who came to the game to sign autographs. The night before Erica graduated, she hosted a talent show that showcased students from the local elementary schools. Erica had set a goal to raise $10,000 by the time she graduated from high school. She had amassed $8,500 when a donor, who wished to remain anonymous, made up the difference.

During high school, Erica was also involved with both the Outreach program and the Interact Club, and because of her volunteer work she received the prestigious Alan Shawn Feinstein scholarship. When Erica went to Rhode Island College, she started a community service outreach group called RIC Angels, through which she continued to host fundraisers for Camp Heartland—ultimately raising twenty-seven thousand dollars. She was also very involved with the campus ministry at Rhode Island College and would spend her spring breaks volunteering at orphanages and homeless shelters in other cities.

After graduating from college, Erica spent hundreds of hours volunteering for CareNet-RI, a Christian pro-life organization (now known as Harmony Women's Care) that supports women with unplanned pregnancies. As a registered doula (birthing coach), Erica would provide guidance to these women before, during, and after their deliveries.

Then, in December 2014, we received the devastating news that Erica was diagnosed with stage IV inflammatory breast cancer, which had spread to her bones. By this time, Erica was thirty-two years old, and with her husband, Joshua, had an eighteen-month-old son named Cade. Even more devastating, Erica was fourteen weeks pregnant with their second child. The doctors recommended an abortion as a way to extend Erica's life.

Erica never considered it. During her pregnancy, Erica endured immense pain. She underwent five chemotherapy treatments, and her care at Women & Infants Hospital took her from the emergency department to the antenatal care unit, to labor, delivery and recovery (LDR), to the surgical services unit, to the acute monitoring services unit, and to the neonatal intensive care unit (NICU). Despite the physical and emotional pain, Erica never lost her faith. She would continually inspire everyone who came to visit her by proclaiming God's deep love for them. When Erica's hair fell out from the chemotherapy treatments, a friend applied henna to the back of her head to create a design that read "Be still and know that I am God" (Ps 46:10).

Erica and Joshua were warned of the uncertainties of her being able to sustain the pregnancy and deliver a healthy baby. Yet on April 29, 2015, against the medical odds, Erica gave birth to a beautiful, healthy baby girl. She and Josh named their precious miracle Eleanor Gianna Shea (Ella for short). The name Gianna was chosen as a tribute to Gianna Beretta Molla, the Italian saint who was diagnosed with a uterine tumor during pregnancy, and died a week after giving birth, having rejected surgery to save her own life at the cost of her child's.

Erica died two months after Ella's birth, mirroring Gianna's selfless gift of life for her daughter. Erica's final act was a perfect culmination of the way she had lived throughout her life on earth, and we see her face daily in her two beautiful children, Cade and Ella, who both have inherited Erica's smile, energy, and determination.

According to the Catholic Bishops of the United States, "Human life is a gift from God, sacred and inviolable. Because every human person is created in the image and likeness of God, we have a duty to defend human life from conception until natural death and in every condition."[1] By the grace of God, Erica understood the importance of defending and protecting human life, and she did everything she could to align herself with the Church's teaching on human life, even when it meant losing her own.

Shortly after Erica passed away, we were made aware of a letter written by Mark Marcantano, the president and chief

[1] United States Conference of Catholic Bishops, *Faithful Citizenship: A Catholic Call to Political Responsibility* (Washington, D.C.: United States Conference of Catholic Bishops, 2007), 17.

operating officer of Women & Infants Hospital, to his staff. The letter shows the far-reaching impact of Erica's decision to choose life:

> Late yesterday, Dr. Ray Powrie and I took to the halls for our monthly executive rounding session. It's a wonderful time for us to connect with patients, visitors, and staff. . . . But yesterday was different. Yesterday, my life, my attitude, my perspective were changed forever. Yesterday, I met Erica, a young woman who recently delivered a beautiful thirty-four-week baby girl. That happens all the time at Women & Infants, right? But this is different. You see, Erica has cancer, very advanced cancer. And the doctors really weren't sure if she would be able to carry a pregnancy and, if she did, if she'd deliver a healthy baby. But she did carry that pregnancy. And she did deliver a beautiful, healthy baby named Eleanor Gianna; they are calling her Ella. . . . On each and every unit [where Erica received medical care], in every hallway, in the cafeteria and lobby, every step of the way, our staff has been amazing, often with tears in their eyes and lumps in their throats. Buying blankets and hats for the baby. Bringing flowers for mom. Offering support for dad. Being a shoulder for other relatives and friends. One staff person I spoke with said that he's never seen anything so miraculous, so intense. He was looking forward to going home, digesting this miracle, and appreciating time with his family. A labor and delivery nurse said it was the most powerful thing that's ever happened to her. A float nurse commented, "This is love. Love is the most powerful thing on earth." Yesterday, when I entered Erica's room, her family surrounded her. Her beautiful baby was lying skin-to-skin on her chest. Her husband, Josh, was stroking her hair, just like a truly loving husband would do. It was inspirational and moving. This is a family —including eighteen-month-old Cade—that is bound by faith, by love, by prayer, and by hope. They asked me to

> pray with them. And I did. It brought me to tears. . . . For a moment, all of the noise, all of the stress, all of the uncertainties were gone. We were Women & Infants again, where miracles happen.

After Ella's birth, Erica was very weak. My Dad and I would bring our guitars into Erica's hospital room and sing to her. While lying in her bed and holding Ella, she would simply move her feet, as if she were dancing, and move her head from side to side with a smile. Music, like love, rejoices with the truth.

I have a video of Erica lying in her hospital bed, her hair short and thin from the chemotherapy, Ella resting peacefully on her arm. Erica turns to her newborn daughter and says, "We will tell the world our story."

Yes, Erica, we will.

Anonymous Twitter User

For my Twitter friends who actually care, I said one day I'd share the story of why I'm so pro-life: I was about twenty-two, I mostly lived to party. I'd get drunk every single night at my favorite dive bar before heading downtown to whatever party or bar was happening. I had nothing going for me. Dead-end job, lived with my parents, barely working car. I probably would have wrapped it around a tree trunk if given a few more years. On my birthday, a bunch of my friends came out, and I got exceedingly drunk. I ran into an old fling, nice-enough girl. We had a one-night stand.

A few months later, I'm working the night shift stocking shelves at a grocery store, and I get a call. It's the girl from my birthday night. She's pregnant.

Damn! I make $9.50 an hour and live at home. What the hell am I supposed to do? Call a guy I know who is a pastor.

He's a pretty understanding dude. Asks me what I plan to do. Plan? I haven't planned a thing in my life, I live in the moment.

He asks me if I want a kid. "Hell no!" He gives me a phone

EDITORS' NOTE: This essay needs a brief introduction. One day we came across a collection of posts on Twitter from a guy with a strange screen name, a vulgar vocabulary (cleaned up for this book), and a deeply inspiring story. It took some time to track him down since his account had since been deactivated, but once we did, he was willing to share his story in this book, but he wished to remain anonymous. Here is what this young man shared with his followers on Twitter one day.

number, says it's a relationship counselor, tells me to call her and explain my situation.

I called her, explained what was going on, and she had a reasonable proposal: Why don't you two come meet me, and we can talk about this in an environment that feels safe and open?

I called Jenna. I tell her that I want to try to be a good person, and maybe we could talk about it with this person who is an expert in bad situations.

First meeting comes and this lady is a little out there, but very understanding. Jenna and I are able to talk about what we want. We come to a tentative agreement that we should get to know each other.

Jenna's dad is a doctor, she's had everything she's ever wanted or needed in life. She's a great student and college athlete. I'm a screwup. My parents, while wealthy, have mostly cut me off and I have an awful relationship with them at this time.

That poor woman at age twenty is faced with several bad choices: hitch her wagon to a fricking deadbeat loser, get an abortion, give the baby up for adoption, or keep the baby and cut me off, finishing school as a single mom.

In what could have been called the worst decision she's ever made, she decided to go with me—a guy who stocks grocery stores, lives in his parents' basement, and drives a car that barely runs.

We started going to couples' counseling twice a week, literally to get to know each other. Now Jenna had never dated anyone before. Suddenly this deadbeat scruff ball shows up with her at all her family events, church, and dinner on Sunday, the whole nine yards.

We eventually get to the point where we decided we

wanted to keep the baby and maybe get married. This is about four to five months into the pregnancy. She hadn't told her parents yet and she was starting to show a little.

Every time we tried to tell them, she'd have a panic attack and we wouldn't tell them. Eventually it got to the point where someone had to tell them or they would guess, and I realized I was going to have to tell them myself. I looked her dad up on his hospital's website and called his office. Asked to meet with him.

Folks, I was not a brave man. I always took the easy way, being a coward and a weasel, but I went to that fricking meeting and broke that poor man's heart. He knew what I was, and now his beautiful, intelligent, sweet daughter was forever linked to me.

Hardest thing I've ever done is telling a good man that I may have just ruined his daughter's dreams, and his dreams for her.

This man is a saint, folks. He took it stoically. He didn't yell or scream or kick my ass. He thanked me for telling him, and said he would be in touch, that he had to talk to his family.

Jenna called me an hour later. She was furious. Called me every name in the book and then some.

Then her mom called me and told me to come to dinner that night. Talk about walking into a bad situation, but I went.

It went great, actually. Her family was supportive of her, wanted to make the best of the situation, and offered to pay for the counseling we were going to ($100 bucks a week is a lot when you make $9.50 per hour).

After a month or two we decided we would get married. Jenna dropped out of school and started sewing decorative pillows to make a little money. I started to get my act together with work. I went from a crap employee to the best dude they had.

I completely turned my life around. I had no choice; it was sink or swim and I had to carry two others on my back. I worked my tail off and got some promotions and small raises.

Out of the blue, my parents made us an astounding offer: they would buy a very modest house for us and would defer payments for the first couple of years of our marriage.

We found a nice house in a safe neighborhood, and they bought it. A month later Charlie was born.

Charlie changed my world. From the moment I found out about him, he began to save me. Charlie transformed me from a directionless screwup to a man with a purpose.

Hindsight is great right? I didn't see it then, but that tiny little human inside Jenna changed me more than any other influencer ever could. He made me be a man, he saved my life, and he brought the love of my life into my life.

So why am I pro-life? Because I understand that a small, seemingly insignificant and helpless human can have a profound impact on the world. Simply by existing, an unborn child has the power to save someone, to radically change a life.

And Charlie didn't just save me, he brought Jenna and me together, and through that came Henry and Annie, two more wonderful, amazing people who will have a huge impact on the world.

A life is never a mistake! The power in a life to save others is immense. It may not be clear at that time, but in time it becomes clear. Charlie saved my life, and I would never want someone to lose that amazing chance.

On a practical note, Jenna's pillow business took off, and

what used to help feed us now helps pay for the kids' school. We eventually bought the house with our own money, and I worked my way up to a supervisor position at a factory, and now manage two hundred people.

My relationship with my parents has never been better. I love my in-laws so much, and Jenna and I are able to help others in need. I can't imagine where I would be if we had chosen abortion. Abortion is an evil thing.

Suzanne Guy

"If there is a heartbeat, there is hope." My mom offered us these words inspired by the Holy Spirit during our darkest hours twenty-two years ago, and they still echo in my mind as a driving force today. The power of one person to breathe words of hope into a desperate situation can never be emphasized enough, for it was this simple statement that took my husband and me from a place of deep sorrow, despair, and inward focus to a place of eyes full-throttle on Jesus, determined not to abandon our daughter to death when she was very much alive. Very sick, but very much alive. Only He can impart that hope into the deepest parts of our troubled hearts. It is He who delights in using others to be His mighty megaphone.

It is hard to believe, as we watch our vibrant, loving daughter, that twenty-two years ago she was given a death sentence by the very people we thought would recognize the intrinsic value of her life. Her life was deemed disposable because of a prenatal diagnosis.

Our daughter's value is not due to her survival, nor because of the happy ending to our ordeal, but because of the simple, beautiful fact that she is a human being made in the image of God.

Our story begins with years of struggle with infertility.

Suzanne Guy, together with her daughter, is co-leader of Marietta 40 Days for Life 365. She founded and heads a pro-life group called Life Initiatives and Values.

After much crying out to God and seeking Him, He brought me to a place of surrender. It was not easy to pry my clenched hands open to surrender my dream of having children, but, as God has a way of doing in His tenderness and patience, He brought me to a place where I could let go of my own plans and give precedence to the Dream Giver who offered another path. God gave me a joy-filled enthusiasm to love other people's children, and I decided to go back to school to be a teacher. After that journey began, what an unbelievable surprise it was when, after years of rushing to the drug store to buy countless pregnancy tests month after month, that little line finally showed up on the screen. My husband and I were elated, and we began telling people immediately. Because of those years of infertility, I was told I needed to go to the best practice with the best doctors at the best hospital. So when I was accepted into the care of a renowned practice, my husband and I never thought to question the referral.

We were shocked to learn that not all doctors value preborn life—especially lives with a poor prenatal diagnosis. Our daughter's only crime was being sick before birth. The doctors not only devalued her life, but insisted it was medically necessary to abort her, stating both of us might die if the pregnancy progressed.

My pregnancy started off fine, but before the end of the first trimester I began to get horribly sick. Every time I called my doctor to tell him how much I was vomiting, he assured me that everything was normal. My mother felt I needed to get an IV right away, but every time I consulted my doctor, he repeated his assurance that I was fine (it was subsequently discovered that I was suffering from hyperemesis gravidarum). Then during one of my prenatal visits, the doctor told me my protein test indicated there was a chance that our baby had Down syndrome. He wanted to do an amniocentesis, but I told him that possible diagnosis did not matter to us, that we would welcome and love a child with Down's, and that we would not risk harming the baby with an amniocentesis. His frustration at that point should have been a major red flag, but my husband and I honestly had no idea that some physicians place judgments on who is valuable and who is not.

My husband and I eagerly awaited our ultrasound appointment at twenty-two weeks, when we would get to see our baby, but at the last minute, my husband was called out of town on business. Being so excited, we decided to keep the appointment and I went alone. Not long after it began, as the technician was moving the wand around my stomach and I was excitedly watching the screen, the technician asked to leave to get a doctor to join us. I knew that was probably not a good thing, but I was not prepared for what was about to happen.

A doctor from the practice, not my primary ob-gyn, came in and frantically started to tell me that my baby had no kidneys, and had a chromosomal abnormality incompatible with life. She then said that half my amniotic fluid was gone and that I needed to abort our baby immediately. Although shocked, I immediately refused, and she insisted that there was no choice, since my life was in danger as well. She and I went back and forth as she explained that my child was not the size she should be for her gestational age, and the abnormalities she saw indicated that the child couldn't survive. I sat there wondering why on earth a doctor would tell me to take my child's life because she may not live. I refused over and over, and in frustration she told me to come back two weeks later.

I left and immediately called my husband in tears, and he reached out to my primary doctor to try to make some sense of everything. The doctor explained to him that my lack of amniotic fluid was nothing to worry about and that I should just drink more water. This absolutely stunned me. Drink more water? I was just told several times to kill our child by the other doctor, and my primary says to just drink more water. This made no sense! I called my mother, who is a strong prayer warrior with a deep love for Jesus, and told her how the one doctor was practically yelling at me to kill our child because she was incompatible with life, and then my primary says to just drink more water. There was a bizarre discrepancy that I could not reconcile. My mom and I began to pray for my baby.

Two weeks later, my husband came with me to the follow-up ultrasound at twenty-four weeks. The same doctor I had seen at the last ultrasound now said I had *no* amniotic fluid. My husband was witnessing firsthand what I endured two weeks prior. The doctor was even more frantic, emphasizing the chromosomal abnormality and saying that even if our baby lived, the lungs would be too premature to be helped. Abortion, she insisted, was the only option. We were devastated. Devastated that someone in the medical field saw our child as disposable, of no value and worthy of death because of being sick in utero. When we refused her recommendation, she sent us to talk to another doctor in the practice. We met with this other doctor, who, for more than twenty minutes, in the most bone-chillingly calm way, insisted that we needed to abort our child. For twenty minutes, we explained why we would never do that. How curious to have to try to convince doctors of the oath they took and of a human being's worth. I literally thought I must be losing my mind or misunderstanding something, as who on earth would ever think they would have to try to convince a doctor not to kill their child?

He offered us a laundry list of medical problems that would impact our child's "quality of life," and in response, we stressed that the child was valuable regardless. He was impervious to our insistence that other children couldn't replace this particular life—which still mattered! The doctor refused to listen, and in the calmest of voices insisted that no one, in his seven years as a doctor, had ever refused to abort.

To this day, I cannot share this story of ice-cold bullying in the face of our profound pain without tears. It was clear at that point that our family had been written-off by this doctor and his practice, and to add insult to injury, when we asked if we might have further testing, we were told that the only test they would provide at that point would be an autopsy.

We went home in deep sorrow and called my mom, who said, "Does the baby have a heartbeat? If there is a heartbeat, there is hope. We pray!"

That put our focus back on Jesus and the great hope that there was still a life to be protected. An ob-gyn friend from church helped us find a new doctor, who was committed to honoring our request to fight for life. He and his colleague valiantly fought for our Rachel, and she was born alive via C-section at twenty-six weeks, weighing one pound two ounces. I remember saying over and over and over, "She is alive. She is alive." She remained in the hospital's NICU for five and a half months and received attentive care from precious doctors, nurses, and therapists who treated our whole family with such kindness—indeed, they became family to us.

Rachel is now an adult, and as difficult as it may be to believe, she is the picture of health.

Rachel does not have a "chromosomal abnormality," and is a living testament to the admonition that no doctor should ever be allowed to instruct parents to kill their child. That said, even if the diagnosis had been correct, it's just as wrong to kill someone for being disabled! Rachel's clean bill of health is just the exclamation point on what used to be an obvious medical truth—*do no harm!*

Since her birth in 1998, I have been deeply concerned not only for the preborn but also for women experiencing unplanned and crisis pregnancies. Rachel's life was used by God to make us aware of the need for each of us to be His voice for these vulnerable individuals who need to experience Jesus' compassion and hope, as her grandmother firmly reminded us.

Fighting for Rachel—before and in the months after her birth—became a cause that, though certainly difficult, brought its own joy. Knowing that we pursued what was good, determined to embrace life for as long as it lasts, has given this grateful family a path to true peace and happiness.

Dean Gavaris

On one side stood protestors from Planned Parenthood and the National Organization for Women, on the other side Christian pro-lifers, and in between were a pregnant woman, her five-month-old preborn baby girl, and county police officers in knee-boots, ready for a confrontation. That no confrontation occurred proved that there was one more presence on that wintry morning in Somerset, New Jersey —the unseen hand of the Author of the tapestry of life.

In the poem "God's Tapestry," Emily Matthews writes "If we but trust Him, even when we do not understand, our lives can be great works of art, designed by His own hand."

Christians know the Author exists, but how can mortal men and women vanquish the unseen forces of darkness? When we unite ourselves to God and allow the Holy Spirit to guide us, the enemy is disabled. To the degree that we relinquish our own will, we are able to see more clearly how God weaves His tapestry of life by using His children to accomplish His holy will.

Reverend Dean Gavaris was ordained to Christian ministry in 1993, and he has worked in the pro-life arena since 1981. From 1986 to 1990, he was the executive director of Archway Pregnancy Center in Elizabeth, New Jersey. In 1991, he founded Gateway Pregnancy Center in Irvington, New Jersey. Dean is a recipient of the Erma Clardy Craven Award, from the Life Education and Resource Network, an African-American evangelical pro-life association. In 1997, he received the Guardian of Life Award from New Jersey Right to Life.

For Sonya Jackson, a woman then in her early thirties, God used the skill of an attorney, Rich Collier, who stated "This baby has an inalienable right to life, and nobody can take that away." He used a judge, Leonard Arnold, who decreed, "I have decided that this unborn child requires representation."

He used the expertise of an activist, William Calvin, who coordinated raising bail and financial support. God used the medical training of an ob-gyn, Dr. Jose Arrunategui, who five years earlier had been an atheist and a second-trimester abortionist. God's grace had changed his heart and his profession. Now he was ready to be used in the tapestry.

Financial help and physical assistance were offered by strangers, all a part of the tapestry.

God also used the timeliness of the local police. A policeman recognized Sonya on the street and arrested her on an old drug charge, incarcerating her two days before her scheduled abortion.

God also used the pleas of a minister who was directing a crisis pregnancy center minutes from where Sonya was arrested.

Finally, God used the confinement of a jail cell and the deception of life's enemy to work His sovereign will. The results were never in doubt, except to those who saw only the disjointed, earthly threads of the tapestry, and not the completed work.

Ordained ministers can go where crisis pregnancy centers cannot, so God prepared my visit to Sonya on a cold January morning.

I first met Sonya on January 29, 1997, when I visited her at the Somerset County Jail. I had been called in by pro-life friends Bill Calvin and Richard Collier. A weary Sonya listened as I spoke to her about fetal development and the consequences of her choices. But mostly I spoke to her about the love of God.

I explained to her the second-trimester abortion procedure and shared with her the gospel, her need for repentance, and the importance of trusting in Christ for salvation. I also outlined the help we could provide for her.

I met with her again at the jail two days later. She seemed excited to see me, not only because of the help she was receiving, but because she had sorted out several things concerning her life and her decisions.

I didn't try to persuade her to save the baby, but simply explained the truth about the baby and about abortion. My goal was to show her the compassion of Christ. If she had the facts and knew of our concern for both the baby and her soul, she would be more likely to carry the baby to term. I offered her all the help of a pregnancy center: counseling, baby items, adoption information, and medical care—all free.

Although I've counseled thousands of women, Sonya still stands out. Her rekindled desire for God shaped her thinking. This was not a jailhouse conversion for the purpose of leniency. Sonya simply responded to the truth brought to her by her new friends.

Sonya told me of her past deeds, including a drug habit that had ended eighteen months earlier, previous abortions and her initial intention to abort this child as well.

"Not one of them asked if I thought about keeping the baby," Sonya told a reporter. "All they talked about was the abortion, that I had a right to have one and no one could stop me." Thankfully, God lovingly spoke to Sonya, and the truth was brought to her inside the jail and subsequently in the courtroom.

This woman had sat in the courtroom handcuffed, silent,

and depressed, and heard attorney Richard Collier's forceful defense of her unseen baby: "This baby is going to a facility where he will be yanked out of the womb and killed outside of the womb. That is infanticide." The description deeply moved Sonya. "I felt this man knew what he was doing," she recalled. "He was fighting for that child. That weighed on me."

The judge had called on Richard Collier because he needed someone who was current with pro-life litigation. God sent the best. A graduate of Harvard College (cum laude) and Boston University School of Law, Collier served two years as a law clerk for a federal judge in Trenton, New Jersey, before spending thirty-six years in private practice.

"The judge showed a basic act of human compassion and a genuine concern for Jackson's baby," Collier noted after the hearing.

When Collier described the suffering a baby undergoes during a partial-birth abortion, Sonya responded that she felt "so ashamed." "The description was so powerful it stuck with me. I couldn't forget it."

As the hearing ended, Sonya's own public defender and an ACLU representative pleaded with the judge not to release Sonya to the "bad influence" of her new friends. "The judge could not believe it," Collier noted. The judge pointedly asked the public defender and the ACLU representative, "Are you telling me you don't want your own client out of jail?"

Although the judge agreed later that day to release Sonya for an abortion, God had a different plan for this baby. There was still the long night of spiritual battle and soul-searching.

The night before Sonya Jackson's release from jail, the forces of evil were at work. Deep into the night plans were made to secretly transfer her for the abortion. She was awakened from sleep around 3:00 A.M. to prepare for the trip, but she would not budge. The unseen Hand was at work in the tapestry of this preborn life.

Sonya's own words reflect the truth of God's intervention. A few days after being released on bail, she described her heartfelt plea for help. "I asked God to help me decide, to send me some sort of sign when I was in jail." Sonya then turned to her new friends, saying, "This is what He sent. They were my sign."

That same night, instead of sleeping, Sonya mulled over the situation—her possible criminal trial, her dismal financial straits, as well as the strain she also faced with the two children she already had. She weighed those factors against the words I had shared with her: "This baby has a right to live."

After the 3:00 A.M. wake-up call by the guards, the drama continued. At 5:30 A.M., a small group formed at the front door of the jail, praying. At 8:00 A.M., a man and two women who indicated they were from the National Organization for Women were at the jail's back door. Sonya was told she would be released to this group, so she could avoid the media gathered at the front door.

Journalist Douglas Campbell described the spiritual tug-of-war this way: "The 'choice' forces were literally at the back door and the 'life' people were at the front, and [Sonya] was being called by both."

Having already made her choice, Sonya wouldn't succumb to the last-minute pressure to destroy a young life. She turned toward the front of the jail and stepped into the welcoming arms of her mother and her new friends.

She was taken to the office of Dr. Arrunategui, where she wept upon seeing the ultrasound of her baby and hearing the strong heartbeat.

Within the space of a few days, Sonya Jackson was transformed from a handcuffed, silent, and depressed prisoner to a happy, hopeful, animated young woman. God had spoken to her, and she decided to listen.

Lacey Buchanan

I was twenty-three years old when I became pregnant for the first time. Although everything at my six-week checkup seemed normal, I sustained a nagging apprehension about the pregnancy. At my eighteen-week appointment, I got the news that something wasn't right. The ultrasound scans did not reveal the actual nature of the problem, however, and my baby continued to grow.

Before my son was born, though, the doctors gently informed me that he was likely going to die. Although the apprehension I had felt prepared me somewhat for the news, it was tremendously painful. I went home and tried to continue with my normal routine of work and school, but the weight of impending sorrow was always with me.

Christian came into the world on a cold, windy day in February 2011. His first breath outside the womb was followed by the loud cry I had desperately prayed to hear. The cry meant he was breathing, and although I was barely conscious on the operating table, I was ecstatic. No one else shared my joy or the miracle present before us. A blue sheet separated me from my baby and the doctors. Their silence

---

Lacey Buchanan is an attorney, author, and passionate advocate for people with disabilities. She and her husband have been married for thirteen years, have two sons, and are also foster parents. Lacey lives in Tennessee and can be found online at LaceyBuchanan.com as well as on Facebook, YouTube, and Instagram. She also offers a podcast, *Pushing Back the Dark*, in which she speaks about her advocacy efforts for her son.

was deafening. No one would give me answers. He was brought to me for a few moments and then whisked away to a NICU and I didn't see him again for about eight hours. When I did see him, he was in a hospital crib, and I wasn't allowed to hold him, feed him, or change him. I was allowed only to sit next to him and look at him. My sweet Christian was alive, but not without challenges. He had facial clefts that affected the formation of his eyes, lips, and skull.

Rather than reveling in the miracle that he was alive and breathing without assistance, the medical staff seemed blinded by his birth defect, which defined their entire thought process. Doctors were constantly saying "I'm sorry" or "We don't know." I never heard "Congratulations on the new baby" or "We are thankful he's alive." Palliative care was offered, but I didn't understand why—Christian was alive! Later I realized the doctors were treating him as if his life were ending.

I wanted desperately to get out of the hospital, which had the somber aura of a funeral home, and get back to living. When that day finally came a month later, I had no idea we would face an entirely new set of challenges from the outside world that would require a considerable adjustment. I had expected to get home and begin moving forward, but at every turn we were faced with someone whose narrow understanding of a disability defined their opinion of a human's worth.

The world outside the hospital wasn't like a funeral; it was more like a bad fortune-teller. People would predict our future with absolute certainty—defeat, misery, suffering, and dejection—and then many would do their part to make sure their predictions came true. Some would stare at Christian and speak about him as if he were subhuman. Posting a picture of him on my social media led to accusations of begging for attention or pity. I was told I was selfish for not aborting Christian and that killing him would have been more compassionate.

Today, Christian is eleven years old. He reads Braille and is learning to play the violin. He took karate lessons for three years and enjoys going on hikes and wrestling with his younger brother, who is his biggest fan. He loves animals and wants to be a doctor when he grows up. His quick wit and sense of humor can make an entire room erupt into laughter. Christian does anything that any other child his age does. He loves who he is, too. Recently, he asked me about his facial difference. When I explained it to him, he said that he wished everyone was like him. He didn't wish that he was like everyone else. I think that speaks volumes about who he is and what it's like living with a disability. I think it also says a lot about those fortune-tellers who thought they knew what kind of future Christian would have. Those who based their determination of Christian's worth on his disability or on how much he wasn't like them ended up being completely wrong. Christian isn't like everyone else, and we're thankful for that. He doesn't want to be like everyone else. He knows that who he is is not a mistake.

His value has always been based on his God-given humanness, his intrinsic worth as a part of the human race, and the fact that he was purposefully, fearfully, and wonderfully designed and created in the image of God.

Joy Villa

Fashion is fun, but it can also express one's personal beliefs and convictions. My statement at the sixtieth annual Grammy Awards event in early 2018 was "Choose life." On the red carpet, I carried a purse with that message and wore a white gown designed by the bridal company Pronovias. On the full ball skirt, I had hand-painted an image of how my own child looked in her sonogram when I was eight months pregnant.

Then, in 2019, I wore a provocative pink latex gown to the Los Angeles premiere of the amazing film *Unplanned*, which is based on the book of the same name by Abby Johnson. She had been a Planned Parenthood clinic worker in Texas but wisely (and dramatically) left that wretched organization behind—and became a pro-life activist.

I called the pink latex gown my "pro-life Barbie" look; it displayed a proudly rebellious message: "F*** Planned Parenthood." As you can imagine, the critics *loved* it!

I received thousands of rape threats and vile comments from people, many of them young teen girls, saying they hoped I'd get raped and die. Brainwashing by celebrities who support Planned Parenthood has been abhorrently destructive to our teenage girls in America.

I also received thousands of encouraging comments and

Joy Villa is a singer-songwriter, an actress, a speaker, and a conservative activist. This article is adapted from her book, *Kickass Conservative!* Learn more about Joy at JoyVilla.com.

letters, many of these from women and girls who were now choosing life over death. I love my job!

My dress ultimately gave the middle finger to Planned Parenthood and to all the radical liberals who keep talking about being "pro-choice." Let's be honest: what they're really saying is that they're pro-abortion. They're in favor of taking human life when that human life becomes inconvenient for them.

I was standing up for life in the most public way I could. And I shared my pro-life messaging very deliberately. I wanted to showcase love. I wanted to shine a bright light on something that celebrities rarely discuss in public today.

I believe in loving the child and the mother, and I am proudly pro-life, without any judgment of others.

More than a decade ago, my own life was shattered.

I learned that I had a beautiful baby growing inside of me. But it was a crisis pregnancy, and I couldn't stop crying. (I shared some of these details in an op-ed published by Fox News.)

For many women in stable, loving relationships, or many women of a certain age or circumstance, becoming pregnant can be and is a dream come true. But when it happened to me, I was at first overcome with guilt, agony, and shame.

I was so young! At age nineteen, I had fallen in love with an older man who was very kindhearted. But once he began using drugs, our relationship became a nightmare for me. In those very dark, challenging times, I didn't know where to turn. I was penniless, far from home, and trapped in a toxic relationship.

When you're young and vulnerable, sometimes your mind plays tricks on you. You think, "I don't deserve happiness" or "I guess this is the best I can do."

It pains me to remember how devoid of value I felt all

those years ago. But for a while, I believed I deserved to be abandoned, forgotten, and punished. I thought, "This must be my fault, so I have to stay and try to fix this." Maybe it was also my stubborn streak that made me think I had to stay the course, figure everything out on my own and make it work.

After a contraceptive failed, I went to a local clinic to get a pregnancy test. And when the pregnancy test came back positive, the nurse began to pressure me to get an abortion —right then and there. *That day.*

She told me, "We can do it now. It's easy. It's free! It'll make it all go away."

She also said, "You're too young to have children. This is the best choice for you."

So, let's get this straight. This nurse, a stranger to me— and someone who worked at the clinic—*was trying to make my choice for me.* Yet she had no idea who I was. She didn't know about my life or my beliefs. She didn't know my heart. She didn't know my head. She didn't know my soul.

I told her no.

And I walked right out of that clinic.

I was scared—shaking, distraught. But no one was going to tell me what to do with my very own baby.

My heart breaks for the unborn and at the horrors and flat-out lies of Planned Parenthood. Abortion is not health care. Babies are living things. They're human beings, *not* clumps of fetal tissue!

No parent ever mourned the miscarriage of a "clump of fetal tissue."

I never considered abortion. *I believed in life.*

I wanted to stay and make things right with the baby's father, to have a real family. And I prayed to God constantly. I knew I was in a bad situation and wanted to make it better.

Then one day when I was much further along in my pregnancy, I was violently thrown against the wall. At that point, I knew I had to take dramatic action.

So, I left to be on my own. My baby deserved so much better.

That's when God gave me the idea of adoption.

I looked down at the table where I was sitting, and a newspaper was lying open. It had an article with the headline "Loving Homes Looking to Adopt."

I made the most difficult and crucial decision of my young life. I decided to carry my baby to full term on my own, then try to adopt her out to a beautiful, loving, kind, and generous family. I chose to put her life over mine.

It was one of the hardest things I've ever done. Every day was a struggle. But it was the right thing to do.

And I would do it all again in a heartbeat.

Pregnancy is difficult, especially without family by your side. The mother's body is growing and changing every day as the child inside her grows.

The way you walk changes over time; the way you breathe changes; the way you sleep changes; the way you interact with the world changes.

Not only is your body nurturing another human being, your understanding of who you are as a human being and what your future holds is changing too.

I stayed with my dad for a significant part of my pregnancy while missing my mom intensely—she had passed away by this time after suffering a stroke. It was a time of tremendous upheaval in my life. Mostly I was by myself, thinking, planning, and trying to stay healthy for my baby.

But my faith in God and my love for my baby gave me the strength I needed to survive. I kept asking God to guide me. *And He did!*

I believe all human beings possess the right to life—that we're given a gift by Our Creator to live and survive from womb to tomb. And I believe that the family is the backbone of society and should be protected, respected, and honored. And that fighting for our individual freedoms is the most important fight of all.

Adoption is an important option that's being left out of pro-life and pro-choice arguments today.

It should not be left out. It should be *prominent* in these discussions.

My baby deserved everything. My child was a gift from God. And I wanted my child to have the best life possible.

And when my beautiful baby girl was finally born, I looked into her sweet face and renewed my commitment to do the very best thing I could do for her.

I found an adoption agency that helped me every step of the way. And I placed my baby with a loving, caring family in an open adoption, which meant I could still be involved in her life.

Forever and always, I love her with all my heart.

I am able to see her. And because of my decision to choose life, I continue, to this day, to have a growing and wonderful relationship with my daughter, who calls me "Mama Joy".

The adoption route gave me—as a terrified young teenager who found herself pregnant—the greatest gift of my life. It gave me a second chance, a chance to do the right thing, a chance at healing, and a chance to be a mom, even if I wasn't going to be the actual hands-on mom of this child.

So yes, at the 2018 Grammys, I was celebrating my beautiful daughter by hand-painting my gown with an image of my child's sonogram.

I didn't care what people said about me. It's *life* that matters most.

I knew the baby I had carried. I knew her intimately.

No one else did!

As Donald Trump said during his presidency, "Every life brings love into this world. Every child brings joy to a family. Every person is worth protecting."[1]

I encourage women in crisis pregnancies to think for themselves and to gather all the information they can before making a decision. Having life-saving options such as adoption can empower women to do what *they* feel is right, not what other people may think is right.

Thousands of women at this moment are in situations similar to the one I was in. And many girls are even younger and far more vulnerable than I was.

I am not here to condemn anyone or to make vulnerable young women feel worse than they might already feel. There's already too much negativity in the world.

But I do have a message—a strong and passionate plea to young pregnant women: Consider adoption for your baby. *Consider life.*

Consider carrying your innocent little baby to term and placing your child with a caring family that will give your newborn all the love and resources your sweet child deserves.

You *will* make it through this experience. You're much stronger than you know. You deserve a second chance at life—and your baby deserves a *first* chance.

Life is precious. And so are you!

I chose life over death for my child. I choose life over death every day of my life. And I have no regrets at all. My choices are part of my life, past and present.

Being a pro-life advocate is something very personal and

[1] "Remarks by President Trump at the 47th Annual March for Life", Archive.org, last updated January 24, 2020, https://trumpwhitehouse.archives.gov/briefings-statements/remarks-president-trump-47th-annual-march-life/.

something that should be done in love. It shouldn't be political, yet for some reason, many people try to twist this topic, usually for their own ends.

I get a lot of negativity about being pro-life, which only shows the hypocrisy of the other side—of liberals, of liberalism, of the left. Here I am, a strong conservative woman and a woman of color, who shares my beliefs—yet the other side tries to shut me down. *Ironic.*

When I was at the One Life March in downtown Los Angeles a few years ago—the pro-life event that celebrates the beauty and dignity of every human life—it coincided with the Women's March that year. And many of the Women's March folks who were out there were so nasty. Some even yelled and screamed at me, telling me I had no right to decide in favor of life.

It's crazy that even now in this country, at this point in time, we have to defend our personal beliefs. We have to fight for our right-to-life positions.

If you're a young conservative who believes in life and who believes in the right to life, I say: speak up about it! Others can believe what they want (although how anyone can go against innocent life blessed by God is beyond me)—but your beliefs are *yours.*

If you fervently, passionately, and wholeheartedly believe that life begins at conception, as I do and as millions of other pro-life Americans do, share those beliefs with others *and do everything you can to live them out.*

Do not allow anyone to talk you into anything, including abortion, if it goes against your most sacred and heartfelt beliefs.

If you're a young woman who finds herself pregnant, please know and remember that *abortion is not your only choice.* The precious life you're carrying within you deserves a chance.

Reach out to others. And don't be embarrassed or ashamed! Human life is always worth protecting.

Believe in yourself and your values. And act on those beliefs.

Trust your heart. Know that you are not alone! *You can do this.*

I know because I was there myself.

And today my child is *alive.*

Michele Linn

I am a hospice nurse. I care for patients who typically have six months or less to live. Some twenty years ago, I was assigned to care in-home for a baby boy named Braden. His story is one only God could write. It is a story of the unwavering faith of a family, the miracle of life, and the unconditional love of the Father.

I was told the baby boy was born with a rare genetic condition called Pfeiffer syndrome (type 2). Not knowing much about this diagnosis, I did a little research and learned these children are born with craniofacial abnormalities, suffer severe neurological deficits and respiratory compromise, and often do not live past eighteen months of age. Knowing what was to come, my heart sank as I prepared for my first visit with the family. As I pulled up to the home, I remember praying for the family. They were admitting their little baby into hospice care and I knew this meeting would be very heavy, tearful, and emotional. As I approached the door, I was greeted by a beautiful young mom with the sweetest smile. She was so unexpectedly joyful and said, "I can't wait for you to meet him, he is so awesome, you are going to love him!" She walked me to his room, and I looked down

---

Michele Linn is a retired registered nurse of thirty-six years. She currently serves as a volunteer spiritual counselor for Hospice of Western Kentucky. Michele and her husband, Peter, have three children and seven grandchildren and are active parishioners at Blessed Mother Catholic Church. Braden West, the protagonist in this story, serves as a volunteer firefighter and does ministry work.

at the most precious baby boy. Yes, he looked different and had significant craniofacial abnormalities, however, he had the same sweet smile as his mom, and it was genuinely love at first sight. I sat in awe as I listened to Braden's parents tell me his story. They had a peace about them, a peace I would later learn is a peace that comes only from God. Their faith was unshaken, and they seemed grateful for every moment they had with him. As I left that first visit, I knew this assignment would be different. However, I had no idea of the journey of faith the Lord had in store for me, and how I would be the one to walk away blessed beyond measure.

Braden's parents, Chuck and Cheri West, learned of his abnormalities two weeks before his due date. During Cheri's thirty-eight-week visit, the doctor discovered she was measuring larger than expected. An ultrasound was performed, and she was told there was "a problem with the baby." The Wests were referred to a specialist who confirmed their fears. Cheri said the physician told them that if they were of the Christian faith, they should go home and pray the Lord will take the baby before delivery. Being high risk, Cheri was scheduled for a Cesarean section. Through many tears, they prayed for God to take him until the moments before he arrived.

On the day of delivery, the nurse said, "You're going to feel some pressure, and then the baby will be out." At that moment, the prayers of her heart changed, and she immediately cried out to God to save her baby. She vowed she would use his life as a testimony if He would just let them have him a little while. Immediately after delivery, Braden was rushed to the NICU, where he would spend the first four weeks of his life. During that time, they were told his chances of survival were slim. At one month, he was discharged home to his parents and big brother Christian so they could love and care for him for whatever time he might have left. He cried in constant pain from increasing intracranial pressure and had surgery at two months of age to remove part of his skull. Shortly after, he underwent additional surgeries to have a tube placed in his stomach for feeding (gastrostomy), and a tube placed in his trachea for breathing (tracheostomy). At three months old, he continued to decline and was placed in hospice care.

Braden's first few months in hospice were filled with many ups and downs. The most persistent concern continued to be his respiratory difficulties. He had developed pneumonia and began having labored breathing and respiratory distress. In hospice care, the goal is comfort, so no heroic measures were to be performed. I was called in for crisis care, which indicates that the patient's symptoms have become unmanageable, death is imminent, or the family is in need of additional support. I was assigned an overnight shift in the home in an attempt to manage his symptoms and keep him as comfortable as possible. As I watched him struggle to breathe throughout the night, I worked diligently to keep his airway clear. I spent the night suctioning, positioning, administering medications and breathing treatments, and holding him closely in an upright position. As the gravity of his condition became more apparent in the early morning hours, I began to cry. I prayed and pleaded with God to please just take him home now or make him better. It was just too hard for him, and too hard for his parents to watch him suffer. I honestly was not sure he would make it through the night.

However, as the sun came up, his breathing became slightly more stabilized. I left feeling grateful but unsure of what the next few days would hold. What happened next is nothing short of a miracle. Braden slowly improved over the ensuing days and weeks. And then, to my astonishment, he began to thrive! With each visit, I was greeted with a new accomplishment or hurdle he had crossed. God had answered the prayers of his parents and so many others who knew and loved him, including me. A few months later, Braden West became the first patient I ever had the privilege to discharge from hospice.

My relationship with Braden and his family continued, however, in a slightly different manner. I checked in on him regularly, attended birthday parties, and had a front row seat as he repeatedly astounded the medical community by soaring past every milestone they said he would never meet. At age five he began to walk, at age eight he began to talk. Despite multiple hospitalizations and more than thirty surgical procedures over the next few years, by the grace of God he recovered from each one better than before.

Braden is now twenty years old and is the kindest, most loving person you will ever meet. To know him is to love him. In high school he was a straight-A student who participated in JROTC and Civil Air Patrol, lifted weights, and got his driver's permit. When he graduated in May 2021, I was honored to be asked to take his senior pictures. While I'm not a professional photographer—just a nurse with a fancy camera—I was not going to pass up such an awesome opportunity. As I drove to their home that day, I kept thinking of how eighteen years ago I had cried because I thought his life was ending, and now I'm crying because he is graduating from high school and his life is just beginning! At the photo shoot, Braden had a few ideas for pictures and the photo most important to him was a picture with his Bible.

As I talked with him during the shoot and over the following days, God's plan and purpose for Braden became so apparently clear. Braden loves Jesus with all his heart. I am not sure I have ever met anyone who loves Jesus more.

He recently told me he was saved in order to "lead people to God and lift people up to Him." He shared that at age seven, before he could even talk, he met God face-to-face. Cheri would later explain that it was during a family vacation that Braden had fallen from their parked vehicle. He landed headfirst onto the concrete and was not responding or breathing. As she was preparing to begin CPR, she asked Chuck and everyone in the lobby of the hotel to please pray. Braden gasped and began to breathe. When evaluated at the hospital he was found to have normal scans and X-rays with no concussion. When Braden finally began to speak more than a year later, he told his parents about going to heaven. Later, as he shared the experience with me, he explained "I saw God and I saw the scars on His hands and feet. I saw the beautiful streets of gold, the beautiful colors, and beautiful trees all around." He said there were others there too. I asked Braden if he recognized any of the people present and he said, "Yes, my great-grandpa and my uncle." I asked if Jesus talked to him and he replied, "Yes, He told me it wasn't time for me to come home. He said I want you to go back and tell people about me and I want you to lead people to me. I promised Him I would. After that I woke up in the CT scan."

When I told Braden how inspiring his story was and how it mirrored other accounts of heaven I had either read or heard about from patients, he was amazed. He told me he didn't know anyone else had experienced what he had. As the tears streamed down my face, I thanked God for the gift of Braden West. The Lord chose Braden. The Lord chose a genetically abnormal, imperfect little boy to do His most important work. The Lord chose a baby the world often discards to show the world a miracle. The Lord chose Braden to give us all hope.

Braden has kept the promise he made. Unapologetically and with much confidence, he tells anyone who will listen about God's love and promise of salvation. Through his ministry Less Worry More Prayer, Braden speaks at churches and schools, spreading a message of hope. I recently asked him if he ever felt angry at God for being born different and he answered, "I'm never angry about that, we are all beautiful children of God, and I am 100 percent His." Braden already knows he is perfect in God's eyes. My prayer is that one day the world will see him the same way.

Daniel Schachle

God has perfect timing. This miracle I experienced is a perfect reminder of that, especially in light of the challenges our nation has faced in recent years. As you read my story, I think you will see what I mean.

Rarely does anything happen in a vacuum. I believe it was divinely inspired that, in 2014, for the first time ever, the Order of the Knights of Columbus decided their annual incentive-award trip would be a pilgrimage. I am a general agent for the Order, a Catholic fraternal organization that provides insurance and financial services and supports many charitable programs. In 2015, Fatima was selected as the pilgrimage destination.

My wife discovered that she was pregnant near the end of 2014, and on December 31 we were told that our son, whom we planned to name Benedict Ives, had Down syndrome. We were not upset by this, and although we knew it would bring additional hardships, we also knew it would be a huge blessing to our family.

Shortly after receiving this diagnosis, I attended the 2015 Knights' general agents' meeting and heard an inspiring presentation. The speaker said that if we possessed God's knowledge of events, we would never question why bad things

---

Daniel Schachle and his wife, Michelle, live in Dickson, Tennessee. They have thirteen children and four grandchildren. Daniel, a United States Air Force veteran, has been a member of the Knights of Columbus for twenty-seven years, and he serves as the Knights of Columbus Insurance general agent for Tennessee, Kentucky, and parts of Arkansas and Virginia.

happen, for we would see how God uses adverse circumstances for our greatest good. Thinking this was reinforcement that my son was a gift, I drew strength from these words.

Shortly after this meeting, the doctors at Vanderbilt University Medical Center informed us that our child had an additional genetic condition of severe swelling known as hydrops fetalis. We were told by the doctor (who assured us that she was raised Catholic and knew how we felt about abortion) that we had only two options: terminate the unfortunate pregnancy now or wait for him to die, leading to a stillbirth. The latter option carried with it the additional risk to the health of my wife, who might develop a condition that mirrored our son's. The doctor insisted that this wouldn't really be an abortion since there was no hope, and because my wife, who was over thirty, was already in the high-risk category for women. Her final argument was that she had never heard of a child surviving this diagnosis.

Obviously, we were devastated, as were our other children. Although my wife charitably tried to credit the doctor for her concern for her well-being, I was angry at her for telling me it was okay to kill my child. I knew that fathers are supposed to protect their children, both physically and spiritually. Everything, including status, money, influence, and comfort, must be set aside when our children need our care.

In our private discussions, having rejected abortion as a solution, we sought reasons to hope. One day when I found Michelle crying, I remember telling her, "I don't know who the hell that doctor thinks she is telling us there's no hope—we're going to Fatima!" One night, as Michelle lay on the floor sobbing inconsolably, I felt desperate. I went and sat in a chair in my room and had what I would describe as a moment like the Agony in the Garden. I didn't want my wife and children to hurt anymore. I didn't want to go through this pain with them. But it was all out of my hands. While pouring all this out to God in prayer, I remember asking for this cup to pass from me if it be His will. And then I turned to Father McGivney and asked him to pray for my son.

This connection with Father McGivney was a natural one for me to draw upon, as I had turned to him many times in the past. I felt he was always with me in my vocation with the Knights as an agent charged with taking care of widows and orphans. I made a promise to him that I would name my son after him if he would pray for him. Although my wife was resistant about the name (she really wanted to name our son after her maternal grandfather), she agreed. Together the next morning, we sent e-mail messages to our family and friends asking them to pray for Father McGivney's intercession to save our son's life.

We were blessed to be awarded the trip to Fatima and first made a side trip to Rome with some friends. We arrived on the day that the Holy Father announced the Year of Mercy, and just prior to leaving Rome, we attended a private Mass in Saint Peter's Basilica. Not only did it turn out to be the opening Mass for the Year of Mercy, but it was offered at an altar that had been refurbished by the Knights over a decade earlier.

We continued on to Lisbon, where we prayed at the birthplace of Saint Anthony of Padua. At the Fatima apparition site, we prayed the Rosary with Archbishop Lori, who was inspired to conclude it by consecrating the Order of the Knights of Columbus to the Immaculate Heart of Mary. At Mass in the Basilica of Our Lady of the Rosary, the reading of the day was from the Gospel of John, in which a royal official begs Christ to save his dying son. Jesus' initial response wasn't encouraging: "Unless you see signs and wonders you will not believe" (Jn 4:48). In his mercy, though, Jesus said, "Go, your son will live" (Jn 4:50). We hadn't told many people on the trip about our situation and didn't even sit in the front of the basilica with those who came to Fatima seeking miracles. Rather, mixing into the crowd, we quietly reached for the hem of His garment, and the Gospel found us there.

Next, we traveled throughout Spain, making many pilgrimages, including one to the tomb of Christopher Columbus in Seville. Throughout the journey, the Gospel from the Mass at Fatima echoed in our minds, filling us with hope.

Upon returning to the United States, we had another ultrasound test that was reviewed by a different doctor. She began to explain to Michelle about the medical team that would be working with our baby when he was born, when Michelle stopped her. "Dr. Mary, what do you mean when he is born? I was told there was no hope." The doctor consulted her chart and asked, "Are you the one who just went to Fatima?" When Michelle said she was, the doctor told her, "Well, now you're going to have a baby." The medical condition that rendered my son's life hopeless had vanished. "Our help is in the name of the Lord!"

I was scheduled to attend a conference in San Antonio in May, and although Michelle was not due until July, I considered backing out. Michelle insisted that I go, since the Order was going to present me with an award. I left Nashville on May 13, the feast of Our Lady of Fatima. On the day I was scheduled to return, May 15, Michelle had a routine ultrasound in which it was discovered that she would need an emergency C-section. Thus, in the Divine plan, I wasn't home in time for the miraculous birth of our son Michael.

Both physicians who had previously attended and counseled us wanted to perform the C-section together, the original doctor admitting that she never expected Michelle to be there. Michelle told her she was so happy to see her, and that she had brought a gift she had been waiting to give her. She handed her a Miraculous Medal and holy water from Fatima. The doctor took off the necklace she was wearing and added the medal to it. "You don't know how much this means to me" was her tearful response. I am told that this doctor keeps the before-and-after ultrasounds on her desk to this day to remind herself there is no such thing as "no hope."

Michael is the youngest of thirteen children, and Father McGivney was the oldest of thirteen. Although this special-needs child was marked by the medical community for death, God mercifully intervened, reminding us that all life is sacred, and He is the author. I am deeply grateful that He used us to remind the world that parents should never lose hope.

Toni McFadden

As a young black woman, I was completely uneducated about abortion. When I, as a high school senior, had to tell my boyfriend that I was pregnant, his reaction was typical for our age: "You don't want to keep it, do you?" My best friend's reaction was similar: "You cannot keep this baby." As far as I could see, ending the life of my unborn child was my only option.

Reflecting on the situation today, I am astounded at how truly misguided I was. Planned Parenthood had accomplished its mission where I was concerned. I'd received their well-marketed message and I was going to do as they suggested: abort my baby without my family being the wiser. I remember sitting in the waiting room of an abortion clinic with my boyfriend across from me and my best friend at my side. Two of the closest people in my life, and yet I felt completely alone.

I wish I could forget the feelings that I had while sitting inside that place. I was about seven weeks along and just wanted this to be over. There were so many girls there, some even visibly pregnant. Were we all here for the same reason? When my name was called, I remember looking at

---

Toni McFadden is an international speaker on the topic of abortion and healthy relationships. She is the founder of Relationships Matter, which seeks to educate youth on the degradation of sex in our culture while equipping them to walk in healthy relationships, protecting themselves and honoring their future spouse. Toni's book, *Redeemed: My Journey after Abortion*, was published in 2022.

my boyfriend as I walked toward the nurse. Up to that moment I thought we were in this together, but he made no move to get up and come with me. With my best friend at my side, I lay on the table so they could give me an ultrasound. I asked the nurse if I could see the monitor, which was strategically facing the wall. Both my friend and the nurse agreed that it would be better for me if I did not look. Not knowing all of a sudden why this was so important to me, I insisted. "See," the nurse said, "it's just the size of a pea. It's nothing." Nothing. In my scared teenage mind hearing that made me feel better. It's not a baby yet, it's nothing. I am doing this early enough, I thought, before it is a real baby.

The nurse never told me that by this time my baby's sex, eye color, skin tone, and height had already been determined within my womb. She did not tell me that at twenty-one days, my baby's heart had already started beating within me. These are the things I wish I had known.

After the ultrasound, I went in to see a doctor. He was cold and direct, and I never thought to ask what he was giving me. I took what I now know was RU486, a medical abortion pill. Imagine taking something and you have no idea what it does. All my life I had gone to doctors when something was wrong and they fixed it. They made it better. Given this trust, there was no reason to think this time would be any different. After I took the RU486, I was given a dose of mifepristone to drink but had no idea what it was or what it would do to me. He told me, "This will stop the fetus from growing." He then gave me two sets of pills (which I now know are called misoprostol) to be taken in the next twenty-four to forty-eight hours.

I walked out of that clinic feeling terrible. I kept thinking, "What did I just do?" The ride home was long as I listened to my boyfriend and best friend talk as if nothing life-changing had just taken place. My primary concern was keeping my family from finding out what I had done, so I went to my friend's house to take the pills. I took the first set of pills and bled a tiny bit. Having not been told this would happen, I called the clinic, only to discover that now their tone was completely different. Where was the kindness the nurse had shown me? Indifferent and unsympathetic, they simply said, "Take the second set of pills, you should be fine. A little cramping and bleeding and that is all." So, I took the second set of pills. Again, I had just a little spotting. I had not been that far along, and I imagined that this spotting was exactly what was supposed to happen.

At some point during this time, unconcerned about what I was dealing with, my boyfriend decided he was no longer going to talk to me. Although he was a year older than I was and already in college, he proved no wiser than I was in dealing with this situation. He never bothered checking in to see how I was, and after a few unanswered calls, I realized he was closing the door on me. My heart was broken, and the grief I had not expected from aborting my unborn baby was choking me, but I had to move on.

A few months later, in the middle of a class during my last few months of high school, I experienced the most excruciating pain. I could barely walk and had to have a friend assist me to the nurse's office. When I made a trip to the restroom shortly after talking to the nurse, I saw blood clots the size of my fist leaving my body. It dawned on me at that moment that the pills had not worked a few months earlier. My mom, who was still unaware of what had happened, came to pick me up from school. When we got home, I went straight to the bathroom, where I passed more blood clots and what remained of the baby. The fear and confusion of the visit to the clinic all came rushing back, and I prayed for this to be over soon. For some reason, maybe God's grace, I cannot remember anything past this point on that dreary day.

I went off to West Chester University and moved through meaningless relationships, college drinking, and what in general I now know to be acting out. To think, I had been seen as the "good girl" in my family. One night a friend randomly invited me to a meeting of a group called Campus Crusade for Christ, and for some reason, I went. Although I had considered myself a Christian prior to this meeting, I discovered through the conversations I had that night that I did not know God at all. I remember heading back to my room that night, crying for God to change me. I was desperate for a change, and I had no idea where to start. God heard my prayer.

I began to blossom in my new relationship with God, and many growth experiences happened over the months that followed. I remember sitting across from a friend at a coffee shop and feeling the heavy burden of my shame. I had kept the secret of my abortion to myself even after finding God because I thought that abortion was the one sin that Christians would not forgive. Something moved me to share my past with her in that moment, to unburden myself of this weight that I continued to carry. She listened carefully. She did not shame me. She did not judge me. As I finished relating what had happened, she said, "Do you know how many girls need to hear your story?" Suddenly, I felt in my heart that this was my purpose, and the conversation led to a job at the local crisis pregnancy center. My friend was already working there, and it was through her that I was able to join this amazing organization. I was tasked with going into schools and speaking about saving sex for marriage, my own regret making me a strong advocate for abstinence. That friend continued to encourage me to share my abortion story with others, and she remains a close friend to this day.

The greatest obstacle to sharing my story with strangers was that my own parents still did not know about the abortion. I found the strength to tell them by looking beyond us to all the young women I would be able to help in the future. Although it was an extremely difficult conversation, sharing the truth gave me a tremendous peace. While naturally they were quite sad, their graciousness was the first major step in my healing. I then started post-abortion counseling, and found a twelve-week Bible study called Forgiven and Set Free, which helped me work through all of the emotions I had never dealt with. This was the first time that I accepted the forgiveness God offered me.

I knew then that God was ready for me to share my story. "Grant to those who mourn in Zion . . . give them a garland instead of ashes, the oil of gladness instead of mourning" (Is 61:3). This verse came to mind as I embarked on the new mission that God had blessed me with. Having washed my guilt in God's mercy, I could work to turn a tragedy into a greater good.

It was during this time that I began to learn more about Planned Parenthood and its targeting of the black community. This modern-day genocide kills black lives every single day, as part of a carefully calculated and strategic plan by Planned Parenthood's founder, Margaret Sanger, and her associates.

I was horrified to discover that Sanger was quoted as stating, at a KKK meeting, "We don't want word to get out that we want to exterminate the Negro population." How had I not realized that almost 80 percent of Planned Parenthood clinics are in low-income, minority areas? My research has given me a passion to educate the black community on the genocide that afflicts us.

I still marvel at the path that God placed me on and wonder at the journey His love has allowed me to travel. I walk this path for Him with an ever-grateful heart. There are so many who need to hear the message of His unending mercy, and I am privileged to be His instrument in sharing it.

As I moved forward pursuing God's purpose for my life, I rarely stopped to think about the early parts of my journey. Little did I know that God was also working His healing hand on that boy who had once sat across from me in the abortion clinic all those years ago. Eventually our paths crossed again, and we were able to share with each other the transformation of our lives through God's love. That same boy, from a seemingly different lifetime, is the man who asked me to be his wife.

Rebekah Hagan

Quicker than I could finish fastening the button on my new jeans, a second pink line began to appear in the window of the pregnancy test, signaling an end to everything I had worked so hard to achieve. This was not one of those sunshine-and-roses scenes you see in commercials. There were no tears of joy, no clapping, and definitely no happy husband to embrace on the day I found out I was unexpectedly expecting. In fact, there was no one there at all, as I sat on the dirty floor of our local grocery store bathroom staring at a bright pink First Response box with neon yellow letters promising "over 99 percent accurate." A fleeting thought arose that maybe the test was wrong—maybe I'm actually part of that lucky almost 1 percent. But I realized it was wishful thinking. At this point, I knew how reliable those sticks were. The test hadn't been wrong when I found out I was pregnant with my son the year before, and, deep down, I knew it wasn't wrong now.

I did not look or feel pregnant. I only took this test to calm my nerves and to ensure that all the loose ends from my previous relationship were completely severed. I had been with my son's father since I was sixteen and he was nineteen. The entire time we were together, I endured physical

---

Rebekah Hagan speaks on the issues of teenage pregnancy, abortion, and abortion pill reversal. She is a graduate of William Jessup University and a mission advancement officer at Heartbeat International. She and her family live in northern California.

and verbal abuse, which I hid from others, telling myself he would change (not knowing that they rarely ever do). One morning during my senior year of high school, while seven months pregnant, I locked myself in the upstairs bathroom, grabbed my MAC Cosmetics "smokey eye" palette and worked for thirty-five minutes to match my right eye to my left. It took layers of black and purple eye shadow to hide the black and bruised eye, but I thought bad love was better than no love at all. Although less than 50 percent of teenage mothers finish high school, and only 2 percent go on to earn a college degree, I wanted to defy the odds. In nine short months, I graduated from high school early, delivered Eli, turned eighteen, and started attending Sacramento State University.

My parents and I had just mended our relationship, allowing my son and me to live in their home rent-free so that I could finish college. They had a few rules that I knew were reasonable, such as maintaining a job and attending classes, not overusing them for babysitting, and, of course, the cardinal rule that my dad made sure to remind me of almost daily: "Don't you dare get pregnant again under my roof." To this he would add, "We've helped you so much the first time that there better never be a second time. If there is, I'll have to kick both of you out." There wouldn't be—I was sure of it. Despite his frequent reminders of all I would lose, my dad's rule was not at all on my mind until my stomach began to feel questionably queasy. I thought it was the stress of all that was happening in my life at the time, but as I watched the second pink line begin to clear, I realized it was more than nerves that had led to my upset stomach.

In the bathroom of Albertsons, I watched my life flash before my eyes. I pictured my parents disowning me, as my dad had threatened they would. I imagined Eli and me alone, poor, and homeless, and me having to drop out of college. There went my dreams and any possible chance of creating a better life for the child I already had—a child whose life had been compromised enough by being born to a teen mom and an unfit dad. Another child, in my mind, would cost us everything and devastate my family. In a moment of panic, abortion seemed like the best way to spare everyone around me from more pain. Despite being a Christian, before ever leaving the stall, I made a plan, telling myself, "God's just going to have to forgive me for this one." The Bible tells believers to pray, discern, and seek wise counsel, but instead, I let fear take over.

I turned to my phone for information and read that there was a quick and simple way to undo the mess I had gotten myself into. It was called a chemical abortion or medical abortion. It was the "abortion pill." It was just medication, which I was grateful for, because having an actual surgical procedure seemed frightening and invasive. Chemical abortion, they said, was more natural and you could even go back to school or work the next day. It was also one-third of the cost of a standard abortion procedure. All of this sounded appealing to a broke college freshman and single mom who needed to hide what she was doing.

On March 13, 2013, I walked into my fourth appointment at Planned Parenthood. Interruptions at three previous appointments had prevented me from starting the abortion process, but today was the day. I checked in, and after waiting for what seemed like hours, I was called into one of the last available rooms in the clinic. Behind a desk sat a nurse with paperwork and a small Dixie cup containing the first abortion pill. She asked, "Are you sure you want to do this?" All I could do was nod, but she needed verbal confirmation. "Yes," I responded. Box checked. At this point, I began to tear up, and I clearly remember her calm voice saying, "You know, Rebekah, just because you're sad doesn't mean you're making the wrong decision." I agreed. Yes, this was crummy, but it was the best of the bad options I had.

The nurse proceeded to reiterate everything I had read online. "This will be very natural, similar to your menstrual cycle. This first pill you'll take is called mifepristone. Mifepristone ends your pregnancy, and once you take it, there is no going back. Tomorrow, when you're ready, you'll take your second medication, misoprostol, and this will expel your pregnancy."

It sounded simple enough. I lifted the cup to my lips and swallowed. She checked my mouth, handed me a brown paper bag—the kind you pack your lunch in—and sent me on my way. I walked to my car, sat down, and tore through the staples to see what the bag contained. As I sifted through it all, grief and guilt consumed me. What did I just do? I don't even believe in abortion. Has my baby already died? Did it feel pain? These were the thoughts racing through my brain as I realized I had just made the worst decision of my life. All I could think to do was pray. "God, if there is a way out of this, please help me find it, and if not, please help me forgive myself." This was the first time I had prayed in weeks.

I grabbed my phone and instantly began searching for a way to undo this mistake. To my surprise, I was not alone. I read multiple posts from years prior, in which women were asking the same question, "Can I stop a medical abortion I've already started?" Unfortunately, every response said, "You must finish what you started. Stopping now is dangerous." I pressed on, scrolling further and further until I found an encouraging website, offering a hotline to women who had taken the first abortion pill and were having second thoughts.

A kind nurse named Debbie answered my frantic call and proceeded to ask me questions none of the abortion clinic workers had asked. "Why did you choose abortion?" "What is your home life like?" "How do you feel now?" and "Do you know how chemical abortion really works?" She explained that the first pill, mifepristone, which I had just taken, ends a pregnancy by starving the growing baby of progesterone, which is essential in pregnancy. I was shocked, but there was more I had not been told. Misoprostol, the second drug, which I was instructed to take the next day at home with no medical supervision, was labor inducing. Women in labor receive this drug to dilate and contract. It hit me. The drugs I had unwittingly accepted would send me into labor at home over the toilet. Tears streamed down my face as I questioned why I had been so uninformed and misled.

Thankfully, Debbie also had hopeful news. A doctor had recently helped a few women reverse their chemical abortion by adding progesterone to their body to counteract the progesterone-depriving abortion pill. She called it APR, Abortion Pill Reversal. "I can't promise it will work," she said, "but it may be a chance to save your baby. If you'd like, I can look for a local doctor to start you on progesterone. Are you willing to try?"

"Yes! I'll do anything!" I exclaimed.

Less than twenty-four hours after taking the mifepristone abortion pill, I began progesterone treatment to try to save my baby. I stayed on the regimen for several weeks. When Planned Parenthood called to see why I never returned to my follow-up appointment—the one where they ensure all of the "pregnancy" was expelled—I told them about my change of heart. They insisted that I was misguided and that if the child survived, it would likely have severe fetal anomalies.

Those were the last words I ever heard from the organization I had mistakenly trusted with the biggest decision in my life. There was no "let us know what happens" or "call back if you change your mind." Planned Parenthood's words haunted me for the remaining seven months of my pregnancy, and I lived on prayer. Still, I was resigned to the possibility of either losing the baby or of having to explain the cause of his birth defects. But I firmly believed that even with defects or anomalies, his life would still be valuable.

And yet, on October 20, 2013, I welcomed another perfectly healthy little boy into my life. I was so grateful for God's goodness and gentleness that I named him Zechariah, which means, "the Lord remembers." Zechariah was one of the first babies born thanks to Abortion Pill Reversal, but thousands have followed. When I said yes to God's plan and yes to choosing life, the future I thought would be impossible turned out to be better than I ever could have imagined. My family not only didn't disown me but offered the help and support that allowed me to finish college on time, marry a wonderful man, and have two more children, Lydia and Jonah. This is our rescue story.

Lisa Wheeler

Blessed is she who believed that there would be a fulfilment of what was spoken to her from the Lord.

—Luke 1:45

I married when I was twenty-seven years old. With my husband and I having received poor catechesis and even worse marriage preparation, we took all possible steps to *avoid* pregnancy. We had never been exposed to the fullness of the Church's teaching on marriage, and we both assumed that birth control was perfectly reasonable for a newly married couple—indeed, that it was a responsible course of action for the success of the marriage. We lived in this ignorance for almost five years, until one day when a priest spoke about marriage in a way we had never heard before. Despite delaying the arrival of children, the time we'd given ourselves to be together as "just a couple" had only revealed that God

---

Lisa Wheeler is the founder and president of Carmel Communications, a full-service Catholic public relations and marketing agency. She has led the Catholic marketing and public relations teams for such film and book projects as *The Chronicles of Narnia*, *RISEN*, *Hacksaw Ridge*, *YOUCAT*, *The Ear of the Heart*, *Fatima*, and *Father Stu*. She also served as coproducer of the film *Unplanned*. Lisa and her husband, Timothy, are passionate advocates for vulnerable children in foster care and have adopted five children over the last ten years of foster parenting. Lisa is a cofounder of Veritatis Splendor, an intentional community for Catholics and other Christians in East Texas that intends, in part, to offer respite and resources to women in unplanned pregnancies and to families providing foster care.

had joined together two deeply opposite people who struggled to find common ground on just about everything.

So, on that providential Sunday, we sat in a parish classroom and listened to this young priest break open the Church's teaching on human sexuality, marriage, and what it truly means to have freedom when you are open to the life that God has planned for you. It became one of the most life-altering moments of our entire marriage. I remember raising my hand and asking the question that changed our lives and transformed our marriage. "Do you mean that we shouldn't use birth control to prevent pregnancy?"

We walked away from that encounter a different couple.

I assumed that I would get pregnant right away once I threw away the pills and got the chemicals out of my system, and yet waiting for that positive pregnancy test turned into weeks. Weeks turned into months, and then months into years. It wasn't until many years later that I learned that all those years on birth control pills likely caused irreversible damage to my reproductive organs.

This began a conversation with God in which I pressed him about why He would profoundly open us to His truth about life, and yet do nothing to help make it a reality for us. I was looking for a promise. One afternoon in adoration before the Blessed Sacrament, He spoke to me very clearly. I questioned Him, doubting His truth as well as His fidelity to me and my future family. He spoke back to me in the words He had spoken to Jeremiah: "For I know the plans I have for you . . . plans for welfare and not for evil, to give you a future and a hope" (Jer 29:11).

Okay, God, bring it, I remember thinking. *But please be quick.*

The years continued to pass, and my circle of friends reflected all that I now believed about marriage and life and love. My husband and I were surrounded by very fertile families, who already had on average six children. The familiar lament of "always a bridesmaid, never a bride" became for me "always a godmother, never a mother."

At a certain point, I found myself avoiding situations that made me vulnerable to the pain of being childless. I began turning down invitations to children's birthday parties and sacramental celebrations, wasn't as quick to offer babysitting to my friends with young children, and avoided toy sections in stores, children's Masses, and any forms of entertainment that reminded me of what I did not and probably would never have. At the yearly Mother's Day Mass, I conveniently withdrew to the bathroom when they prayed over mothers and I left before the obligatory flower giveaway and the "most children" congratulatory gift basket. I had come to my own "dark night of the soul" and had begun to believe that not only had God abandoned me, but that He had dropped me in a Church that mocked me for my infertility. I had lost hope.

As I tried to pray through this darkness, I was led to the passage in Hebrews that reminds us of what faith really is. Paul tells us, "Now faith is the assurance of things hoped for, the conviction of things not seen" (Heb 11:1). I was rational enough to know that I could not see my future, even though I longed for it, but I was also emotional enough to know that my heart needed a break from its all-consuming desire. It was essential that I restore my faith in God's promises.

For the next few years, I poured myself into my work as a publicist for good works in and for the Church. My agency promoted the work of many beautiful apostolates such as the Eternal Word Television Network (EWTN), the Fellowship of Catholic University Students (FOCUS), Educating on the Nature and Dignity of Women (ENDOW), Word on Fire, the Catholicism Project, Ignatius Press, and the Augustine Institute, among many others. Those were years of deep fruitfulness, and I rarely thought about my empty hands. My husband and I traveled the world, engaged in missionary work, doted on our godchildren, and raised furry friends. I had redirected my desire for motherhood into apostolic work, and it worked—for a while.

It was during this time that I sought to draw closer to Mary, the Mother of Jesus, by asking her to journey with me for the rest of my days. And most importantly, I reminded her that I wanted to be a mother too.

Many years earlier, Tim and I had explored the idea of adoption, visiting several private adoption agencies and attending various lectures. Ultimately, and for reasons only he can articulate, Tim was never comfortable with the idea of private adoption, whether domestic or international. Since each discussion made him increasingly negative toward the whole idea, I eventually let go of the possibility. I was resigned to the fact that if I wanted a child, I would either have to get pregnant or receive a basket on my doorstep with my bundle of joy in it.

On one spring day in 2011, as a lector read the announcements at Mass, one jumped out at us: "If you've ever considered adoption through foster care, please read in today's bulletin about an informational meeting being held next week."

As we got into the car, my husband said to me, "So do you want to go to that meeting?" I was stunned. Even though this was different from private adoption of infants, I figured the door was long closed on adoption. I tried not to get too excited and responded, "Sure, if you want to. Up to you." But inside, the hope rose.

The next week we went to our first informational meeting. My heart was burning as we listened to the presentation. And my husband was hooked. Many months later, as more temporal signs were revealed to us, we realized the significance of that first meeting date, March 25, the feast of the Annunciation.

By June, we had completed our classes and turned in all of our paperwork. We had been poked, prodded, questioned, visited, fingerprinted, and held under a microscope. Then we waited. And waited. We had been told we would hear something within a couple of weeks, but it had been a couple of months and we had heard nothing.

In what probably was meant as a consolation, a friend who knew intimately of our journey, and the fact that I saw this as our last hope, spoke some words that pierced my heart. She said she felt that God was telling her that maybe Tim and I weren't meant to have children, and that our fruitfulness would be through our work for the Church and our role as godparents to so many.

In that moment, I went to that dark place of all those years ago, when I felt betrayed by a God who makes promises He doesn't keep. I prayed in earnest that night, asking God why He was taking us through this process only to break our hearts again. I went back to the talk years ago by that young priest who had stressed the need to be open to life, releasing my husband and me from a contraceptive mentality. He had talked about the family as the protagonist in a culture that had lost its soul, and how faithful families could build civilizations of love as Pope Saint John Paul II used to preach, by encouraging vocations and sending forth young people who respected the dignity of life, honored the sanctity of marriage, and promoted peace and justice in a world in which people had lost respect for one another.

So, I begged God with a promise. I promised Him that if he allowed Tim and me to parent foster children, that we would be "open to life" through this nonbiological means by accepting as many children through foster care as He was willing to provide. And that we would introduce these children to Him and to Our Lady, planting the seeds for faithfulness that could potentially last them a lifetime—whether or not they became our forever children.

Not long afterward, I received an e-mail that would change our lives forever. The subject line read "Picture of EMC".

I don't know why, but when I saw those initials, my heart started pounding. I knew without any doubt that I was about to open up the e-mail that would reveal the face of our daughter. There were six words in that e-mail and an image of the most beautiful child I had ever laid eyes on. The six words: "Meet your little girl, Elizabeth Marie." Butterflies erupted inside of me, as God in all His goodness, in all His mercy, revealed that His timing is never late. It is never early. It is always right on time. And most of all, He is faithful in His plan for our lives, because He sees not only our past, present, and future, but the past, present, and future of every other human being who is meant to have a Divine appointment with us.

Elizabeth became an official part of our lives at exactly 3:00 P.M. on December 8, 2011. I'd like to say that our adoption journey was without struggle, but things worth doing are never without challenges. It took nearly two years to journey with her through a very broken foster care system. On May 31, 2013, the feast of the Visitation, the knots were officially untied for her adoption, and in December, the month that celebrates the Divine Infancy, we finalized her adoption.

The fullness of our story doesn't end with Elizabeth. My

husband and I have parented more than fifteen children through foster care. Most have had their families restored through successful reunification or have gone on to live with biological relatives. For some in urgent circumstances, we have provided only respite care, but all have shown us that joy and suffering can exist in the same space when you are open to life.

We made a promise to God in exchange for His fidelity. We would welcome however many children He wanted for our family and do our best to instill in them a love for their Father in heaven. On the feast of All Souls in 2015, we finalized the adoption of our son Malachi. And on September 29, 2020, the feast of the Archangels, we finalized the adoption of Brantley Raphael, Sora Michael, and John Joseph Gabriel, whom we fostered for over four years before they became a permanent part of our family.

Parenting children who survive both what brought them to foster care and foster care itself is not easy. It is certainly not the plan for parenting that I imagined when I got married, but it is clearly the plan that allows me to see the fullness of God's grace at work in the world.

The children who call me Mom were born to other women who were unable to parent them. The magnitude of that tragedy and the depth of that privilege are with me every single day. There is a great line in the movie *Return to Me* when one of the main characters realizes what God has done in her life. Her life is saved, but there is an extraordinary twist that occurs, and at one point, she cries to her grandfather, "What was God thinking?" He responds, "It's the character that is the strongest that God gives the most challenges to. Consider it a compliment."

Living life to the full demands trust. Whether your choices and challenges involve family size, contraception, unplanned pregnancies, or infertility issues, consider it His compliment of you and your character. Had I had been given children when I wanted them, I might never have had my divine appointments with Elizabeth, Malachi, Brantley, Sora, JJ, and all the children we have parented through foster care. The brokenness in each of our stories brought us together so that something greater could be restored.

Almost a year after Elizabeth came to live with us, I received a mysterious package in the mail. It was addressed to me, but there was no return address. Inside was the most extraordinary painting of the Visitation that I had ever seen. It depicts an almost glee-filled image of Elizabeth with her eyes raised toward heaven and her hand placed over Mary's belly. Mary is clutching Elizabeth's hand and smiling. The painting portrays the moment just before Mary proclaims her Magnificat, when Elizabeth says, "Blessed is she who believed that there would be a fulfilment of what was spoken to her from the Lord" (Lk 1:45).

My life today is not easy. This journey has been challenging, but it has also been rich and blessed because I've clung to the hope that God does surely have a plan for our lives and our future, come what may.

Serena Dyksen

When I was thirteen years old, I became pregnant after being raped by an uncle. My parents were devastated, and yet the only help offered to them was to pay for me to get an abortion. At that point in my life, I had never heard the Word of God, and all my mom could think about was how much trauma I would have to suffer raising a child conceived in rape. Our family was not told the truth about abortion. We were offered misplaced compassion that left our family shattered.

An appointment was made at an abortion clinic operated by Dr. George Klopfer. Staff members told us to walk in quickly because the people outside the clinic hated the people who went there. I remember my mom saying, "They don't know what we have gone through. They don't understand." But as it turned out, no one was standing outside the clinic on the day of our appointment. I have often wondered whether the presence of just one caring, compassionate person would have changed the trajectory of our lives.

I remember noticing how dirty the clinic was as I lay on the table, a traumatized thirteen-year-old. George Klopfer

---

Serena Dyksen is an author, a speaker, and the founder of She Found His Grace, an abortion recovery ministry that helps both women and men. Serena speaks at churches around the country to help women and men find their voice through discipleship, and to raise up leaders to champion the pro-life cause. Serena lives in Indiana and has been married to her high school sweetheart for twenty-eight years. She's a mother of four and a grandmother as well.

walked into the room, smiled, and said, "This won't take long." I don't recall being offered any medication. All I remember is a loud noise followed by pain so intense that I screamed and the abortionist yelled at me to shut up. Years later, I read my mom's journal entry from that day—she could hear me screaming but they wouldn't let her comfort me.

When the procedure was over I was taken to a "recovery" room filled with other women. All of us were seated in nasty vinyl recliners. No one spoke. When it was time for me to go home, I started to bleed profusely. The staff not only didn't ask Dr. Klopfer to check me; they insisted that I leave immediately. My dad literally lifted me up and draped me over his shoulder, and we departed out the back door of the clinic.

Our family wanted to forget what happened that day, but we could not. My mom ended up having a mental breakdown and had to be checked into a psych ward for two weeks. I was completely numb, as the abortion trauma only added to the previous trauma of having been raped. Once I came to realize that abortion ended the life of another person, I was completely sick over it, feeling unworthy of my own life. Soon I began drinking. I often tell people the abortion was worse than the rape. I could not help what was done to me, but I would forever live with the knowledge that the innocent life within me had been terminated.

When I was sixteen, I thought I might be pregnant again. Planned Parenthood had an office in my school, and in my naïveté, I believed I could trust them. My boyfriend and I were directed to a clinic in a sketchy neighborhood, and once they confirmed my pregnancy, they told me that because I was young, still in school, and poor, I should abort my baby.

My boyfriend was a Christian but had grown up in a family that had never discussed abortion. He asked me what I thought about it. He was completely scared and to him it seemed like a quick fix that could be kept secret, but having gone through it before, I knew I couldn't do it again. This was the first time I shared the story of my rape and abortion, and I told him I could never end another life. He looked at me with compassion and said, "I don't know how we will figure it out, but we will." And that day, in the parking lot of Planned Parenthood, we chose life.

We were scared to tell our parents and we didn't have anything figured out, but we chose to see this unplanned pregnancy through. Telling our parents was not easy at all. Despite their initial shock, they and so many others helped us learn the parenting and life skills we needed. We are deeply grateful for all their support that allowed us to finish high school and start our married life.

When we were twenty-three, with two small kids in tow, we bought our first house and thought we were beating the odds. Then I suffered a miscarriage and subsequently, one of my ovaries ruptured, nearly causing my death. At the age of twenty-nine, I had to have a complete hysterectomy. At that point, I didn't connect the condition to my abortion, which I still kept hidden as a shameful secret.

In my thirties, my life began to fall apart. With the marriage increasingly troubled, I moved out of our house and planned to file for divorce. At the core, I still felt unworthy to be a mother and wife. I was drinking every single day and not functioning well at all. I was lost and broken and did not know where to get help.

One night I had gone out drinking, and quite unexpectedly I experienced the presence of God, who met me in my brokenness. It was in that moment in my car that I truly felt

His incredible grace, love, and mercy for me. I went home that night physically, spiritually, and emotionally renewed.

My parents and I had no idea how much an abortion would affect our lives, nor of the long journey ahead of us to come to a place of healing. So many people have misplaced compassion, believing that abortion will help after rape, but as I can attest, that choice only added more trauma to my life.

Tricia and Scott

My husband, Scott, and I had been trying to start a family for several years, but after two miscarriages and my doctor telling me I would not be able to carry a pregnancy to full term, we began to lose hope. We stopped talking about having a family and put all our energy and focus into church work and lavishing attention on our nieces and nephews. Then in April 2015, everything changed. In meeting our great-nephew, all those parental instincts and emotions came flooding back. A few weeks later, Scott asked whether I would be interested in adopting. Having thought that door was completely closed, I responded yes in tears, and we began the search for an adoption agency.

In June 2015 we filed the paperwork with an agency, purchased a crib, set up the nursery, passed our home study, created our profile book and waited . . . and waited . . . and waited some more. Adoption usually requires a long wait and patience is essential. After almost two years of waiting and not a single interview, we again began to lose hope. We came to the conclusion that if we did not find a birth mother on our own, adoption was probably not going to happen. A week after saying this, we got the call that would forever change our lives.

Tricia and Scott have been married twenty-five years and love being parents. Tricia studied at Davenport University, and Scott is a graduate of ITT Technical Institute. Tricia is passionate about acting and dancing and has performed in three dinner theaters. Scott loves hunting, golfing, and being outdoors.

A friend from Scott's workplace was dealing with struggles of her own. A young, single mother of three, Lisa was working multiple jobs to get by and becoming increasingly desperate and depressed. After a suicide attempt, her father felt it was necessary to place her children in foster care. A few months later, Lisa found out she was pregnant with another child, after having been raped by her ex-boyfriend. She was ashamed and embarrassed and did not want anyone to know. Hiding the pregnancy from her family and friends, she sank deeper into depression.

Desperate and afraid, she planned to terminate the pregnancy, but then one evening, by the grace of God, she made a decision that would forever change all of our lives. Having heard at work that Scott was interested in adoption, Lisa had previously offered to share our adoption profile in case anyone she knew had an unexpected surprise. Never did she dream it would be her own baby we would be adopting.

On August 25, 2017, Scott was on his way home from work when he received a message from Lisa through Facebook. She asked how our adoption process was going and whether we would be open to adopting a baby from someone we knew. Scott responded that we were still waiting and that if she meant adopting her baby, he did not see a problem with that. Lisa disclosed that she had been raped and had considered ending the pregnancy, but when she thought of our desire to adopt, she couldn't go through with it.

Scott was so excited that he almost got in an accident trying to get home to tell me. He decided he couldn't wait another minute and pulled into a parking lot to call me. I began crying and gave him an enthusiastic yes! When he got home, we called Lisa immediately to discuss the details and get the ball rolling. After the paperwork was completed and signed, Scott and I found out that we were actually the top choice of most birth mothers utilizing the agency, but due to the way we had filled out our paperwork, we were never presented to them. (We had expressed in the application that we didn't want to adopt from a family with a history of mental illness—by which we meant severe conditions like, schizophrenia—and this had unknowingly closed off anyone who was even suffering from depression.) And yet, we now see that God's hand was in this too, because if another child had been placed with us sooner, Lisa might have gone through with the abortion and Kyndal would not be here.

Since I had not met Lisa, we made plans to meet for dinner and get acquainted. With Scott out of town, my first meeting with her would be on my own, and I was a nervous wreck. I kept thinking, "What if she doesn't like me?" or "What if I don't like her?" "What if I say something wrong and she changes her mind?" So many possibilities were going through my mind when I pulled into the parking lot and Lisa pulled in right behind me. We got out of our cars and introduced ourselves, and as soon as we started talking, I was completely at ease! I felt like she was my little sister, and we formed an immediate bond. We talked for hours, never even touching our dinners.

I gave her the information about our adoption agency, and she was to call to set up a meeting with our agent to get her paperwork started. Initially, Lisa said she wanted a closed adoption, in which the records are kept sealed, but since her three other children would be Kyndal's biological siblings, I was open to them meeting her when the time was right. We kept in touch throughout the rest of Lisa's pregnancy and met up a few more times to finalize the birth plan. Lisa was to call us as soon as she went into labor so we could take her to the hospital. Since she still had not told any of her family or friends that she was pregnant, I wanted to make sure she didn't go to the hospital alone.

At 4:13 A.M. on Saturday, October 7, 2017, the ringing of my phone roused us from a sound sleep. Scott jumped up and said, "That's Lisa!" (I had set a special ringtone for her). I answered and Lisa said she was at the hospital and that her contractions were only a few minutes apart. I told her we would be right there. She said that it could be a while and we did not need to come, but I could tell she had been crying and I told her we were on our way. We immediately called our adoption agent, grabbed our bags, and headed to the hospital.

We were not allowed to see Lisa until our agent arrived, which seemed to take forever! Once Cathy was present, we were taken to our hospital room (the hospital gives the adoptive family its own room), and within five minutes of settling in, a nurse came to get me. A few minutes later Kyndal was born; Lisa and I hugged as we both cried uncontrollably. I was able to stay with Kyndal as the nurses cleaned her up and then placed her under the heat lamp. As I looked at this precious baby girl, the realization hit me that this was my daughter! My heart was so full at that moment that I thought for sure it would burst. I texted all the family, telling them that she was here, and as I was holding my hand over her; she grabbed my finger. I was head over heels in love with this baby girl, *my daughter*! Since Lisa had tested positive for Group B strep, Kyndal had to remain in the hospital to be monitored for forty-eight hours, so Scott and I remained with her in our room.

Finally, on October 9, 2017, we got to bring our sweet baby girl home—goodbye sleep! Now the wait began for the adoption to be finalized so Kyndal would be legally ours.

Although we were reasonably certain that everything would be all right, we still had that small fear that Lisa might change her mind, or that something unexpected would happen. I was loving motherhood, but I felt that the bubble could burst at any moment. Then one morning I woke up with the chorus from "The Voice of Truth" by Casting Crowns running through my mind:

> But the voice of truth tells me a different story;
> The voice of truth says, "Do not be afraid!"
> The voice of truth says, "This is for My glory"
> Out of all the voices calling out to me,
> I will choose to listen and believe the voice of truth.[1]

I was immediately at peace—God had this! A week later I received a call from our adoption agent with the finalization date. On March 7, 2018, we arrived at the courthouse and the judge announced that Kyndal was officially our daughter. We celebrated this great day with close friends and family and felt relieved; this precious baby girl we held in our arms was now legally ours! I knew from the moment she was born that I was her mommy, but this just made it so much more real. I could not love this beautiful little girl more if I had given birth to her myself.

> Not flesh of my flesh,
> Nor bone of my bone,
> But still miraculously
> My own.
> Never forget
> For a single minute:

[1] "The Voice of Truth", track 3 on Casting Crowns, *Casting Crowns*, Beach Street, 2003.

You didn't grow under my heart,
But in it![2]

I had worried that Lisa would sink back into depression once Kyndal's adoption was final, but she told me, "Instead of the guilt I thought I would feel placing Kyndal for adoption, I actually feel good. I know that she is loved, and you and Scott are giving her all the things I could not, and that gives me peace." These words put me at ease, and knowing she had peace made me feel better. A couple years later, Lisa was able to reclaim her other children from the foster care system, and she has continued the hard work of putting her life back on track.

Perhaps our story will provide hope, not only to those who are wondering if God will ever answer their heartfelt prayers, but also to those who may be considering terminating an unwanted pregnancy. Many loving families are waiting to adopt, and their courage and patience will be rewarded in seeing how God can arrange marvelous solutions from the most difficult circumstances. Please choose life, and remember, God is always faithful!

[2] Fleur Conkling Heyliger, "The Answer", *Saturday Evening Post*, April 5, 1952, 93.

Genevieve Kineke

I had often heard the phrase "the tears sprang to her eyes" but had never seen it happen before. Now, while lying on a table undergoing an ultrasound, I witnessed it firsthand in my obstetrician and my worst fear was confirmed. My baby was dead. Worry had started nagging me two days earlier as I lay down to sleep after a long day. This was usually the time when the babe would become active, but there was nothing. Then came the slow realization that I couldn't recall much movement in utero at all lately.

I lay awake for a while, waiting in vain for some action. Rising quietly without waking my husband, I slipped into my clothes. A quick trip to the emergency room would clear up this question by confirming the babe's heartbeat. The doctor and nurse on duty warned me that they weren't experts at this, and that if they couldn't find the heartbeat it wouldn't mean much. After a little too much goop and a little more fumbling, each took a turn and found virtually the same beat. I returned home somewhat consoled, knowing my seven-month check-up was just two days away.

Genevieve Kineke is a convert to Catholicism and a widely published author who has dedicated many years to the study of God's generous and intriguing call to women, focusing on the topic of forgiveness as a path to joy and freedom. She founded *Canticle Magazine*, published articles in *Catholic World Report*, *Our Sunday Visitor*, and *Inside the Vatican*, and authored several books, including *The Authentic Catholic Woman* (Cincinnati: Servant Books, 2006). Find out more about Genevieve Kineke's work, including her books, at feminine-genius.com.

But the monthly exam brought the ghastly news—our child was dead. We had two choices. The first was to go home and wait for labor to start naturally; the second, and the only plausible option for me, was to pack a bag and be admitted to the hospital for an induction. After a little time together with my husband to let the new turn of events sink in, we braced for the next step.

Meeting our other four children waiting excitedly outside the examination room wasn't easy. Ultrasounds had always been a family affair—entertaining events we anticipated eagerly, with the souvenir photos displayed on the fridge for months. This time the event was canceled abruptly, and the children walked to the car in quiet shock.

We arrived at the hospital within hours, with a firm resolve to begin and end the ordeal as quickly as possible. What made our arrival more difficult was seeing the same nursing staff we had met less than two years earlier when our youngest daughter was born. Numbness carried me through until we were given our room—the same room as our last delivery. That was a bit much, and our regular doctor, upon arriving, swiftly and gently made the necessary changes so that we were not only in a different room but far away from the nursery as well. Who knew how babies could make one feel at such a time?

The procedure began with the dreaded Pitocin, a labor-inducing drug that, surprisingly, had no effect at all. It was continued through the afternoon and evening and then prostaglandin was applied right to the cervix for the night. (My obstetrician seemed surprised that I knew what this was, but anyone familiar with pro-life literature in recent times knows of this drug.)

After a good night's sleep, the Pitocin was reintroduced and its effect, combined with the prostaglandin, was potent.

Labor commenced, and the pain was intense. It seemed as though my body was fighting the process all the way, knowing the time was not right. But the drugs pried open what the body defensively tried to clamp shut, and I endured the battle with more than this child on my mind.

The timing was too precise for me not to consider an added dimension of my ordeal—for it was the end of the first week of September 1995, smack in the middle of the United Nation's Conference on Women that was taking place in Beijing, China. So many pro-life people had worked hard on position papers, presentations, networking, lobbying, and the like. I was designated as a point person for our people at the conference to relay their feedback to the appropriate media and to keep certain channels of communication open throughout the ten-day event. Now it seemed as if God were saying, "Thanks for all your efforts, but what I need is a little suffering."

In that light, with my suffering so closely related to what we were working for—namely, the freedom of women to choose motherhood and the freedom of children to be born—I felt called to embrace this particular cross for a greater good. I thought of the women going through abortion, especially late-term abortions, surrounded by the same drugs and paraphernalia that were around me, and I wept. They had either chosen this option themselves—having taken leave of their senses—or it was forced upon them against their will, and the thought of that was more than I could bear. I graphically centered on these women's sufferings and what had transpired to bring them to the table, perhaps with straps to tie them down, broken in spirit and crushed physically.

This distracted me a good bit until the pain finally won. The nurses had promised from the start that they had a drug that would not only kill the pain but take the memory as well. This had horrified me, for if the memory of this babe's delivery were lost, what would be left? That was all I would have by which to remember the child, so I figured the drug was not an option. As I say, though, the pain won. It was ferocious, unbearable, and wholly unnatural. I begged for the drug.

I remember the hands on the clock as I asked exactly how long it would be until the medicine took effect. I had to know how many more contractions I'd have to endure. I stared at the clock, willing the hands to move, and suddenly they were pointing to the awaited time and the pain was gone. (I never doubted that my guardian angel kept me alert from that point forward so that the precious memory would be intact.) A full hour had passed and I couldn't feel my body from my shoulders to my knees, yet, gloriously, I was fully conscious. I asked if I could push at this point and after checking the dilation, they said it was time—but could they call the doctor over from across the street? They could order a pizza for all I cared. I couldn't feel the slightest pain.

When the doctor arrived, I prepared to push, and he prepared us for what to expect. I will be forever grateful for his gentleness and sensitivity, letting us know what to look for, what the child would look like, and other details to soften the difficult arrival. My husband caught the babe upon delivery, as he had caught our previous four, yet this time all the usual sounds in the room were hushed. No piercing wail, no hurrahs from the nurses, no congratulations all around—just a reverent calm as the child was received and the details of honoring her brief existence were anticipated.

My husband baptized our daughter Margaret Rose with a bottle of holy water we brought from home. As soon as possible, the lights were dimmed, and the staff left us alone to visit with this little one, with us for so short a stay. We passed her back and forth as we drank in every detail, trying to memorize her features and the bittersweet joy of the moment. Finally, I said, "It's so hard to believe that this is the vehicle for an immortal soul. Do we really believe?" After a moment we each affirmed that we did indeed believe. In that lay the foundation of our whole faith. Until that moment, it had never really been tested; until that moment, the Creed was an abstract body of words waiting to take precise form in this particular circumstance. Yes, we truly believed.

The rest of the day was uneventful. I slept and read and passed the hours comfortably enough, smiling inwardly a little at the staff who were very solicitous of my needs—to the point that I wondered whether, out of curiosity, they all didn't just want a quick glimpse of the "grieving mother." In such a small hospital, events like this were rare, and there were few opportunities to witness how tragedies are dealt with. I'm sure I passed as "heroic" in that short span, but in truth it was sheer numbness that gripped me and allowed me to carry on.

When our other four children were born, my husband's attachment to them was immediate; he did indeed catch the little ones and kept them for most of the first day. In contrast, my connection to them deepened more gradually, and my experience with our fifth baby followed a similar pattern. My usual initial calm reserve was heightened by the unnatural experience, a whirlwind change in a seemingly normal pregnancy.

By the second day, though, I yearned for my daughter. I wanted her desperately and there was no end to the tears—just an aching, empty space by my side, and the realization that now I could no longer hold her. It was over before it had scarcely begun. There was one steady nurse with an ample shoulder, and it was given generously. She was a mother. No other words were necessary; indeed, none would have sufficed. She was just there.

The burial followed a few days later, and it was by far the most difficult part of the whole ordeal. I was obsessed by the "container" used on such occasions. Due to the size of the deceased, instead of a wooden coffin, a glorified sturdy cardboard box was used—literally with a lid like a Christmas present. No seal, no hinges, no latches—just a cardboard lid. It was my only focus at the graveside service and my thoughts ran wild. I could still toss in some rosary beads, shroud her in the family christening gown, give her a memento of some sort, or just whip off the lid for one last peek—or a hug? There was no time, and I knew that I didn't want to see her at that point of closure, but such a rationale didn't erase the bizarre thoughts. Without the forbidding seal on the box, all sorts of possibilities presented themselves.

I was completely distraught and virtually collapsed as the ceremony ended. The sobs came from the depths of my being and the wrenching reality of death. The severance of physical ties was driven home in an agonizing way. I was fully alive and thus completely swallowed by the harsh separation of death. This flesh of my flesh, beneath shovelful after shovelful of earth, would become food for the worms, in cold dark death. That was the deepest abyss of my pain—for after that came the merciful graces of healing.

I can honestly say that the first gift was the Word of God. It may sound like a cliché, but the Scriptures truly did come alive. They nearly jumped off the page. As with the Creed, the imagery was no longer abstract, but completely alive. The words were indeed Spirit and Life, and sweet consolation. God is truly with us and His Word is the promised sword, excising the extraneous that and cutting us to the quick for our greater good.

I also felt God's presence with us, giving strength in this ordeal and proving His constancy and fidelity. As a woman open to life, hoping for a good handful of children, I had always had a nagging feeling in the back of my mind that my number would someday be up. Many women have suffered a miscarriage or lost a child later in one way or another. *How on earth would I be able to deal with it?* I'd always wondered. Well, I learned, you just deal. God moves in and provides the strength to carry on.

It was as though God was teaching me with baby steps since in all honesty this cross was a relatively small one. It wasn't as painful as the death of an older child would have been for me, or as hard as any number of more tragic circumstances. I also had the tremendous consolation of other children to return to. This cross felt soft and gentle and contained—and it was the baby step I needed in the faith to trust that God would be there for the bigger crosses too.

Friends near and far were wonderful and considerate. I was amazed at their empathy since few had suffered this particular loss. Their words and gestures were lovely and perfect. I learned from them, and now know that any acknowledgment is enough. It wasn't what was said but the mere recognition that sufficed. (Silence from a few was painful—how could I be full and round one week and slim the next with no child? But I took it as a lesson and I pass it along in that light.)

I was also very surprised at the number of women I hardly knew who rushed to embrace me and let me know of their understanding. Their losses were varied and painful and it helped to put the events into perspective. There is an incredible amount of suffering in our midst of which we have little clue. I sensed and experienced a special fellowship that exists among mothers who are grieving for lost children. And I'm ever more thankful to God for His own Sorrowful Mother, who understands and consoles us in such difficult times.

Just knowing that people were aware of my loss was enough. Daily Mass was easy because of the intimacy with other attendees, but Sunday Mass the first week was overwhelming because I was surrounded by strangers. I wanted to stand on a pew and shout, "Do you know what I just suffered?" Then shamefacedly I realized that I didn't know or care much about what the woman next to me may have suffered either. Charity had given way to self-pity that day.

Since then, there has been only one really difficult day. In the week following the burial there was a rain shower one afternoon and my first reaction was gladness. We had been lacking rain for so long and this was welcome indeed. The cheer turned almost immediately to an overwhelming grief as I realized that our Margaret was out there, a mile or so away, completely untended. A wave of distress consumed me—much like the frantic feeling when a good book or keepsake is left outside in the elements. But there was nothing to be done. We are composed of body and soul and will not be truly at peace until what death severs is fully restored—no matter how strong the faith.

I pass her grave often and offer the familiar prayer we say when passing every cemetery. But no matter where I am, I feel closer to her spiritually than a physical proximity to her grave can provide.

My only immediate difficulty was settling into an easy answer for those who asked how many children I have. Certainly there was no need to be maudlin with people I hardly knew. Time took care of that awkwardness and despite more losses, eventually another child was born, whose arrival seemed to cover the previous years with a patina of joy. We all retain a bond with Margaret, asking for her intercession, including her in the family lore, and one day, God willing, we will meet her and understand a little more about the value of that particular cross in the eternal plan.

In the year following her death, during the Easter season, I meditated on the invitation of Christ to Saint Thomas to probe his wounds, and my own small wound came to mind. Our Lord's nail marks had previously been a source of great pain, but after the Resurrection, they could be scrutinized liberally, for the good of another, without any discomfort to Him. In the same way my wound has also healed, and I find no pain in retracing it. I humbly offer it to any with an interest, as another reason to praise the infinite wisdom and gentleness of our loving God. Knowing that a mother's greatest privilege is the ability to co-create with God and her husband—to populate heaven—I rejoice that one of mine is already there. I believe she cares for us greatly and takes an interest in the unborn and in suffering mothers. And I have complete trust that all the crosses we willingly embrace are used by God for the restoration of His kingdom.

Paul Aurelius

After many years of marriage, my wife and I rejoiced at the news that she was pregnant with twins! Our doctor recommended we find a physician who specialized in high-risk pregnancies, and we secured the name of the best one in the area. Moreover, the babies would be born at a hospital to which obstetricians from all over the country sent their most complicated pregnancies and which had one of the nation's highest-rated NICUs.

Ultrasounds are frequent in high-risk pregnancies, and my wife got one almost every week. Viewing the babies so frequently helped us get to know them even before birth, and at that time, we referred to them as Baby A, a boy, and Baby B, a girl.

Unfortunately, six weeks into the pregnancy, the doctor saw something in the ultrasound that he didn't like, something about blood being where it shouldn't be. Shockingly, within a week or so, we were told, "Baby A might die in the womb." As bad as that news was, the doctor informed us that with a twin pregnancy, it is virtually impossible and extremely dangerous to remove the deceased child without incidentally losing the healthy baby. In other words, Baby A had to live in order to save his twin sibling.

Paul Aurelius is a child of God, and God isn't finished with him yet. He tries to evangelize everyone he meets in some way. He asks for the readers' prayers.

When the babies were about four months old, the situation was looking dire. With every ultrasound, Baby A was getting harder and harder to see because the diminishing amniotic fluid in his sac was affecting the resolution. Baby B was doing fine, growing and thriving, but Baby A was struggling to survive, with his heartbeat getting weaker and his growth falling behind.

As we understood it, Baby A had one particularly important mission at this time: to survive long enough to save his sister's life.

It is hard to put into words how we helpless felt during this time. We were at the mercy of an outcome completely beyond our control. It gave us a glimpse of what our lives have always been: truly in the hands of God.

As we continued to talk with the doctors about our son's condition, we learned that babies with this syndrome usually miscarry and if not, they certainly do not survive outside of the womb. Now five months into the pregnancy, the doctor repeated, "At this time in the pregnancy, one baby doesn't miscarry without the other baby miscarrying."

It didn't look good. But we prayed and did our best to surrender our wills to God, and in a way, to our unborn son.

Our daughter's life would be saved only through a heroic feat. I thought to myself, "Can a person be a hero before he is born? Does he know God's will? Does he have his own free will? Does God want this baby to share in our Lord's eternal life at such a young age? Does our tiny son somehow understand that this other presence beside him is someone he needs to protect?"

We were quiet about the prognosis, not wanting to worry the grandparents. My wife had been on bed rest since the first sign of trouble at six weeks gestation.

The survival rate for a baby with our son's condition was only 2 percent. "Two percent, two percent" echoed in our ears as we cried in bed that night.

The doctor rattled it off so nonchalantly, or maybe it just sounded that way to us.

We hung our hats on that 2 percent. Over the next few days that 2 percent was just as good as 99 percent to us. Everything was going be just fine, we told ourselves. We could not wrap our heads around the fact that our little fellow was not going to survive outside of the womb. Despite the doctor's offer of further testing to try to determine specifically what was wrong with Baby A, we declined. We would accept our child's fate no matter what illness or conditions he had.

My wife fought to keep any possibility of him dying from her thoughts as she lay on a couch, doing everything she could to protect her children. She knew these babies. She felt every elbow, foot, butt, and hiccup as they grew, and she made it as far as thirty-two weeks when premature contractions began.

The doctor had planned to deliver the babies by C-section at thirty-four weeks, which was the earliest the surgery could be done safely. Already the stress and pressure were taking a severe toll on Baby A. Without enough amniotic fluid to act as a cushion, give him room to move, and to build up his lungs, his heart was not strong enough to battle the weight of the pressure on him. And now, despite medication to prevent contractions, it seemed that birth was imminent. I was out of town for work, so my wife had a friend take her to the hospital immediately.

Soon after she was settled into the hospital, I arrived and secured a room at the adjacent hotel. (Little did I know that that hotel room would be home for the next month.)

My wife was in the hospital bed with two heart monitors around her belly—one monitor showing a normal rhythmic heartbeat, the other showing the heartbeat of a baby in distress. The contractions had been stopped by means of a cervical cerclage (stitching to prevent premature birth), and the doctor ordered two steroid shots to be given two days apart, trying everything to ensure two live births. These shots would boost lung development in our daughter, who now weighed roughly five pounds, as well as give her a speedy growth spurt. Our son weighed only three pounds.

As the weeks went by, with doctor visits and ultrasounds, bed rest became a way of life for my wife. She knitted blankets in anticipation of the babies, although the anxiety and stress she endured must have been excruciating. There was no baby shower, but she had some good friends who sat with her daily, and together they talked and read as the days passed.

A date was set for the C-section, and on that morning, the cerclage was removed.

This would be our moment of truth, the culmination of months of anxiety, hope, and fear.

We were in the labor and delivery operating room. I have never seen so many medical personnel in my life, perhaps as many as thirty comprising every specialist and their teams. They were prepared for any situation that might arise.

The incision was made across my wife's lower abdomen from hip to hip. A drape was placed across her chest, partially blocking our view of the doctor's work. I was worried about my wife and the babies. My wife was concerned about me. She thought I might pass out! One doctor, near the head of the bed, jokingly said. "I'm here to take care of him."

There was tugging and pulling, and the doctor called

out, "Baby A time of birth?" Someone yelled, "11:59!" He quickly handed Baby A to a nurse, who whisked him off to the adjacent room. The grimace on the doctor's face when he handed off the baby was a look I'll never forget. He immediately went back to work, while requesting supplies and speaking in medical terms to the team. Then he exclaimed, "Baby B—it's a girl! Time of birth?" Someone yelled, "12:01!" and then asked, "Was the first baby a boy or a girl?" The doctor said with dismay, "I didn't notice."

My pulse was throbbing in my temple, and my knees became weak and wobbly. Here was the most experienced high-risk obstetrician in the area and he didn't notice? How can a doctor deliver a baby and not notice the sex? The medical team was carefully stitching together my wife's incisions. Reality was setting in. "I didn't notice, I didn't notice" kept resonating in my head.

An order of morphine was prescribed for my wife. A doctor from the adjacent room came over to me and said, "Come see your son."

That was the first time I knew I had a son, and I went in to meet Spencer.

I'm crying as I write this, seventeen years later. His head and face were beautiful with blonde hair and pink skin. He was lying on his back, intubated to keep him alive. His torso was flat as well as his hips and legs. His hips were folded to one side and his legs were angled unnaturally. The doctor opened Spencer's hips that were flat on each other. Yes, that was my son. In addition to the obvious physical deformities, the doctors were not sure what else was wrong. They told me they had to order some blood work and other tests. Then there was an uncomfortable moment of silence. I said some words I'll never forget, words I regret. You see, I was a different man then, not yet appreciative of my Catholic faith, and living a very secular lifestyle. I uttered, "I'll make a sailor out of him."

There was no prayer, no crying out to God for mercy, or even yelling at Him in anger. There was an aura of spiritual indifference. It was all incredibly sad.

My wife was wheeled over to the recovery area. She was sleeping, heavily sedated. She had not gotten much sleep in the past few days, and I had only catnapped. Between exhaustion and shock, I was in a daze and my wife was out cold. As I sat next to her bed, minutes seemed like hours, and hours seemed like days. Doctors and nurses came in and out of the room. I cannot remember exactly what they said, but there seemed to be confusion and conflicting messages. Now, as I reflect upon that time, the discussion was where, when, and how this baby was going to die. A nurse boldly spoke up and said, "This baby should die in his mother's arms." She asked, "Do you want him baptized? Are you Catholic?"

"Yes," I said.

"May I baptize him while we are waiting for the priest or deacon to arrive?"

"Yes," I said again, grateful that for the first time someone brought Him into the room.

She knew the gravity of the situation. I wish I could thank her now for her compassion and thoughtfulness during that critical time.

The doctor arrived with Spencer in a glass enclosure. A nurse was with the doctor holding a portable respirator. The Catholic nurse baptized him. The doctor explained, "He has no kidneys, poorly formed lungs, and other issues. He has Potter syndrome." He went on to say, "We can keep him alive for a couple of days on life support, but he's going to die. There is nothing we can do."

With a focused gaze, I watched Spencer's chest heave in an unnatural way, from abnormally formed lungs being mechanically inflated. My wife was still asleep from the sedation, and a decision had to be made. It was a decision that I wanted to be spared from having to make, but I knew better. The doctor stoically said, "If we remove the support, he will die shortly after."

The doctor explained, "He is not in pain; he is comfortable."

The priest arrived and baptized Spencer again. My body trembled as my voice managed to whisper, "Remove the life support."

We shook my wife and woke her up. Spencer was wrapped in a blanket; his beautiful face was exposed. We placed him in her arms, she kissed his handsome face, and he died in peace.

His mission was complete.

We held each other with Spencer between us, for what seemed like a long time. My wife does not remember much of that day because of the morphine and exhaustion. She learned of some of the details much later, and some more details as I write this.

We were exhausted and in shock. While my wife was sweating, I was freezing cold. Time seemed to be at a standstill. I don't remember the hospital staff taking Spencer, although, of course, at some point they did. Hours later, while sitting next to my wife's bed, a sudden realization came over me, "We have a daughter!" She was on the floor above in the NICU. It is difficult to describe the feeling I had. It was surreal.

I went up to the next floor to see our daughter. Strict instructions were given to wash thoroughly before entering the NICU. Walking past the empty nurse's station, I sensed an unusual aura and I felt as though I were in some sort of dream. There were lots of incubators around the room and one flat table with a baby lying on it. I was drawn toward that table and the baby, who looked like Spencer—and going closer, I saw that it was Spencer! Only his face could be seen. He was covered with a small, thin veil, but why was he there? Every other baby was alive. Am I dreaming? A nurse stood a few feet away, looking at me without saying a word. She looked angelic, dressed in white, and wearing a white hat. Even though I knew the answer, I foolishly asked, "Is he dead?" She nodded. I never saw her or Spencer again. Despite being in that unit for the next three weeks, seeing every nurse multiple times, I never saw her again. To this day, I ponder that moment, wondering if she was some kind of apparition or angel.

A nurse in scrubs came over to me and led me over to our baby girl. Having one child in the NICU and one child in the morgue meant that the saddest day and the happiest day unfolded simultaneously.

Funeral arrangements had to be made for Spencer. I called a priest and told him a little about Spencer. After a moment of silence, the priest said, with a quiver in his voice, "He is a hero." Surprised that he used the word hero, I had to hear it again!

"Father, what did you just say?"

He cleared his throat and said with enthusiasm, "He is a hero!"

At the funeral the priest mentioned our phone conversation and told the small gathering of family and friends about our hero. "Our Hero" is etched in stone on his tomb. Spencer lived a great life because he did the will of God: he saved another person, was born, baptized, and died a natural death with an immortal soul. He had no time to sin. He is in heaven—an uncanonized saint! His mission on earth ended the day he was born, and on that same day my daughter's began.

Spencer, my son, pray for us!

Joseph Scordato

It was the autumn of 2003. Maureen and I excitedly stared at the ultrasound screen. Any preview of our fourth child was a welcome treat, but today was special. We gripped each other's hands, and I kissed her golden hair, nearly tearing up, struck in amazement by her loveliness and motherhood. I loved this woman beyond anything I could say in that moment. We were going to see our baby, and this time it would be with one of the new 3D ultrasounds.

It didn't matter to us that we had been sent to Rockford Memorial Hospital's Maternal Fetal Medicine Center so they could check out a potential issue with our son's kidney. It was the only medical center in the area that had high-resolution 3D ultrasounds. We knew he was going to be okay. This was just a simple check that our doctor wanted us to have.

Early in our marriage, we had miscarried our first child after only eight weeks. My wife named our baby boy Lee, as an acronym for Love Embracing Emmanuel. I recalled the joy we felt at our first-ever ultrasound, hearing Lee's heart beat and actually seeing it on the screen! A few weeks later,

---

Joseph Scordato, with his wife, Maureen, is a Secular Franciscan who are blessed with seven children. Together with Maureen, he produces the *Catholic Family Stories* podcast in which the family dramatizes original stories Joseph has written for his children. The Scordato children, under the name Emerald Wind Music, perform as a musical group throughout Wisconsin and Northern Illinois. The Scordato family was named the Archdiocese of Milwaukee 2020–2021 Family of the Year by the Knights of Columbus.

however, we returned with concerns about the pregnancy, and the doctor confirmed our suspicion that Maureen had miscarried. The following day at work, I was overcome with an unexpected and confusing emotion I had never experienced before. Weeping at my desk, I clutched the ultrasound picture of our beautiful Lee, and the memory of the perfect rhythm of his heartbeat throbbed in my gut, driving home the loss.

Lee's name was one of the first to be etched on the new memorial at Calvary Cemetery for children who had died through miscarriage. The doctor told us that a miscarriage was the body's way of rejecting a baby that had something wrong with it, and yet I knew that God doesn't make mistakes. We knew that it was good that Lee had lived, even if only for a few weeks in the womb, and we looked forward to seeing him someday in all his perfection with the Father.

God gradually healed the pain of our loss as new children were born: Emily, MaryKathleen, Joey, and now our fourth, who we named Christopher. The 3D ultrasound was amazing. We laughed and smiled, seeing our beautiful son so clearly. What a marvelous peek into his hidden world! The technician captured a few pictures, and then snapped another for us just as our son appeared to bow his head and clasp his hands together as if in prayer. My wife and I marveled over this picture as we waited for the doctor to review the ultrasound and provide her report. In a few minutes, she appeared.

"Hi, Mrs. Scordato, I am the doctor on call today. I see that your doctor sent you here to get a better picture of something he found in the recent ultrasound in his office."

"Yes, this is my husband, Joseph." Maureen motioned to me, my hand gently holding her shoulder, while she held the ultrasound picture we had just been admiring.

"Hello." The doctor briefly acknowledged my existence. "Mrs. Scordato, there is a problem with his kidney."

"What sort of problem? Is it life threatening?" I asked.

"It's hard to tell; he could be born without a functioning kidney."

"How is his other kidney? Is there anything special we need to prepare for?"

"His other kidney is fine. I know this can be difficult, but you have options. In such cases, I recommend an abortion."

My wife and I were incredulous. Did she really just say that? Just after our hearts were gushing over seeing our son? I could sense my wife's fighting Irish welling up within her. There was no way in the world anyone could talk us into murdering our son! We composed ourselves. The photo of Christopher praying in the womb was even more meaningful in light of this doctor's advice.

Maureen responded sternly, "Umm, that's not something we would ever consider." The doctor was visibly surprised.

"Oh, I see. Well, whatever. I was just trying to help."

"I don't understand. Why would you recommend an *abortion*?" I asked.

"Well, he's . . . he's not perfect. Why would you want a child that's not perfect?" She shrugged her shoulders.

We continued to be amazed at what we were hearing. We both exclaimed, "He's perfect to us!"

The doctor left in a dismissive huff, mumbling something that was probably best we didn't hear.

Due to the high-risk pregnancy, we were instructed to return each month to check on Christopher's progress. Thankfully, we did not encounter that same doctor again. The follow-up visits required only a technician, until our last visit when we were told that the doctor wanted to see us. We were escorted to a separate office and relieved to find a different doctor this time. He was a thin, middle-aged physician who seemed to carry some administrative importance at the center.

"I wanted to see you before you left. Please take a seat."

His office was relaxing. The lights were dimmer and less harsh than the typical clinic fluorescents

"Thank you," we replied.

The administrator casually walked toward us and leaned against a counter. He crossed his arms, hunched his shoulders, and towered over us in our seats.

"Before you go . . . I understand this is a delicate subject . . . but I wanted to remind you that you have some options."

"What do you mean?" I cautiously asked.

"Well, I wanted to remind you that you have the option to have an abortion. In situations like this, it is a preferable option."

Maureen stared at him in pity, thinking, "He is so clueless—a lost soul." But I went into Dad-engineer inquisitive mode. What was with this place? Every high-risk pregnancy in the Rockford area went to this center.

"Wait. I don't understand. What is so wrong with my child that you think his life should be aborted? Even if he loses a kidney, he still has another. Aren't there lots of people who have only one kidney?"

"Well, yes."

"Don't they live normal, wonderful lives?"

"Yes, of course."

"Then why are you recommending an abortion?"

The doctor replied smoothly, "Now, I'm not specifically recommending an abortion, all I am saying is that it is a good option in this case."

"But why? You said yourself that he will live a normal life

—and even if he couldn't, we would never consider ending his life anyway."

"I am just saying that, if there is something wrong at this stage in his development, there may be something worse later on."

"Did you find something else?"

"No."

"So, you're recommending we murder our child because of some unknown trouble he *may* have in the future, of which you have no indication?"

"Well, you don't have to take my advice, but I am a doctor. I see I won't be able to change your minds, but it's policy—I have to say it. I have to offer it as an option." He waved his hand dismissively as if to say neither our thoughts nor our son's life were meaningful. He abandoned his prey.

We both sat in shocked silence as the doctor completed some paperwork. I had to say something.

"He is our child. If some trouble did occur later, my wife and I would handle it together."

My wife grabbed my hand and we quickly walked out of the office. "Purely demonic," she would later tell me in reflecting upon the event. We stopped by the reception desk on the way out and inquired how we might lodge a complaint. We filled out the complaint form and dropped it into the nearby suggestion box. Both of us were struck by the thought that there must be something particularly good and special about our son that there would be such attempts on his life before he was even born.

Two years after his birth, he did receive kidney surgery. We declined the recommended hormone therapies to increase his height, and subsequent genetic tests revealed that our son was completely normal. Of course, they were all wrong. Christopher is not normal—he's perfect. He has since been joined by siblings Christiana, Nicholas, and Cecilia, and together, we continue to celebrate Lee's life as our special family intercessor in God's embrace. Underlying our great joy, though, lies the disturbing question raised by Christopher's prenatal diagnosis. My question for abortion advocates is this: How many perfectly healthy children have been killed in your efforts to exterminate children with disabilities?

Paul Darrow

Even before she fully understood her challenges, Mary began searching for solutions. She felt she was living a shameful nightmare, just as when she was repeatedly molested in a dank tuberculosis sanitarium at the age of five. Still haunted by that secret, Mary was now burdened with the secret of being a pregnant, unwed teenager. She was as ashamed of her pregnancy as she had been of the sexual abuse.

Neither Mary nor her boyfriend had any idea she was carrying his child when she sneaked out of his apartment and disappeared from his life forever. But now that she knew, Mary asked herself the same questions many of us ask ourselves at some point in our lives: How did I end up like this? What could I have done differently? How will I get out of this mess?

Having very little money and feeling desperate, Mary decided to the easiest way out of her predicament would be to have an abortion. But the more she learned about the illegal back-alley procedure, the more fearful she became. Her

---

Paul Darrow moved to Manhattan right after graduating college and lived as a pleasure-seeker, an international fashion model, and an atheist, embracing the gay lifestyle for several decades. A series of grace-filled events led to a radical conversion. After becoming Catholic, Paul became the subject of the film *Desire of the Everlasting Hills*. He has appeared on EWTN and is a frequent guest on talk radio. He is a member of Courage International and a recipient of its Annual Service Award. Paul shares his unusual testimony to groups across the world in order to be a living example that God's grace is more powerful than even the greatest of human temptations.

concern was not about the baby in her womb, it was about the pain she would have to endure during and after the potentially life-threatening procedure. Her anxiety about the pain was so great that she procrastinated for months about making an appointment with an abortionist.

Just when Mary finally found the courage to go ahead with the procedure, some information provided by a friend altered her plans. A couple in Pennsylvania had adopted a baby boy two years earlier and were looking to adopt again. Mary's friend encouraged her to go full-term so that she could give her baby to them. Although mentally prepared to go through with the abortion, Mary was grateful to have an option that would allow her to avoid the pain and risks of an illegal procedure. She decided to contact the couple.

Knowing very little about the people she was about to meet, Mary trustingly boarded a train that took her to the hills of Pennsylvania. When she arrived, Paul, his wife, Helen, and their two-year-old son, Joey, were waiting for her at the station. Mary's apprehension about being alone on a secluded rural property with complete strangers was soon replaced by gratitude. Paul and Helen treated her well, and she appreciated their offer to stay in their home for the rest of her pregnancy. She spent much of her time playing with little Joey and getting lots of rest.

As the time for her delivery approached, Paul convinced Mary to pretend to be his wife in order to avoid the typically difficult and lengthy adoption process. He had already arranged for a doctor to go along with his scheme.

Even though Mary was only eighteen and Paul was forty-one, the hospital staff believed they were married. The baby arrived on schedule, and everything went as planned until the time came for Mary to hand over her baby to Paul. Unexpectedly, her motherly instincts kicked in, and for the first time since becoming pregnant, she wanted to keep her baby. Overcome with emotions she had never known before, Mary felt she was about to give away a part of herself. But she had already signed the adoption agreement and she believed there was no turning back.

Filled with sorrow and regret, Mary kissed her newborn baby goodbye. To make matters worse, Paul was so anxious to have her depart that he convinced the doctor to release her before she was strong enough to travel. He drove Mary directly to the train station and gave her a new dress, fifty dollars, and a hug. Mary was exhausted, nauseated, and overcome with grief when she boarded the train. Sobbing quietly, she curled up in her seat and drifted off to sleep.

Mary just made it to her room in a run-down Coney Island hotel when she started to bleed. Frightened and too weak to move, she had no idea what to do. Between the hemorrhaging and bouts of agonizing pain, she thought about the mistakes she had made over the last two years. Mary wanted to blame her former boyfriend for what happened, but knew she was responsible for the choices she had made. She regretted leaving her mother's home to search for love and freedom in New York City. She regretted the affairs she had had, and she regretted giving her baby away. Mary also regretted turning her back on God. Believing she was on the brink of death in that dreary hotel room, she cried out to Jesus that she was sorry. She begged Him to take away her pain and save her. Mary promised God she would change her life, and she prayed until she passed out that night. When she awoke, the sun was shining through her window. The bleeding had stopped, and her pain was gone.

Two months later, Helen was surprised to find a letter from Mary in the mail. She wrote that she was well, and that no one, not even her own mother, knew about her pregnancy. She mentioned little Joey, but there was not one word in the letter about her own baby boy. From what she wrote, Paul and Helen assumed that they would never see Mary again—and that Mary would never again see baby Paul. Their first assumption was correct, but not the second.

Mary did her best to follow through on the promises she made to God. She changed her life, married a wonderful man, became a devoted wife, and gave birth to a daughter and another son. Even though she and her husband slowly drifted away from church, she never stopped being thankful to God. Mary was happy and her life was blessed. But years later, her happiness was shattered in an instant when she learned her twenty-three-year-old son, Luke, had been killed in a car crash. Life seemed to stop for Mary and her husband that day.

I was almost thirty years old when I learned that I was adopted. Against all odds, I found Mary forty-two years after she had kissed me goodbye in the hospital. From the first time we heard each other's voices on the phone, we started to form a special bond. That was when Mary discovered I was still alive and that my name is Paul. By our second phone conversation, I was calling Mary "Mom." But in some ways our bond was more akin to a close, loving sibling friendship than to the mother-son bond I had with the mother who had raised me. I told my widowed mother Helen that I knew about the adoption, but I never told her about finding Mary. I did not want her to mistakenly believe my relationship with Mary would ever diminish my love for her.

Mary told me things about her life that she had never shared with anyone else. She told me she prayed for me and felt there was always a little part of me in her heart. She also described the profound effect Luke's death had on her and her husband. After his accident, Mary could not stop thinking about how she had given one son away, and God had taken the other. Knowing of my existence helped her cope with her ongoing grief over Luke's death. She said she might not have recovered from losing Luke if she had chosen abortion over adoption for me.

Luke had been the pride and joy of Mary and her husband. After he died, they were unable to eat or sleep or even talk to each other. They tried sleeping pills and different antidepressants, but nothing worked.

They both fell into a deep depression, and Mary believed she was on the brink of a nervous breakdown. Her feeling of desolation reminded her of the hopelessness she had felt years earlier when writhing in pain in the Coney Island hotel room. Remembering how she had prayed back then, she went to her husband and said, "We've tried everything else, maybe we should try going back to church." They went back to church, and in the ensuing weeks, the oppressive weight of sorrow gradually lifted from their shoulders. Their lives slowly returned to normal, and church remained a permanent fixture for the rest of their lives.

My mother Mary told me there were three events in her life that most solidified her relationship with God. The first was giving me away in the hospital, the second was losing Luke, and the third was finally reconnecting with me so many years later. Ironically, it was these overwhelmingly painful, sorrowful, and regretful experiences, along with the joy of having me back in her life, that increased her love for God and helped her to fully embrace her Catholic faith. It is such a blessing for us both that Mom chose life for me, and that we were so lovingly reunited.

When facing a decision between choosing an abortion and choosing life, choosing life will almost always seem like the more burdensome choice. But as I learned from my mother and from many other women, ending the life that God chose for you to bring into the world is the most burdensome choice a parent can ever make.

Brad Smith

"Starvation is not a medical treatment, overdose is not a medical treatment, and death is not our daughter's cure."

We begin each of our daughter Faith's first appointments with new physicians by making these statements. Faith is thirteen years old and has Trisomy 18, also known as Edwards syndrome.[1] We have learned over the years that in the medical community there is an ambiguous value assigned to children like Faith, who have both mental and physical disabilities. This can lead to vastly different standards of medical care. Thus, the responses to her medical needs vary widely, depending both on the physician and institution, as well as the level of knowledge and advocacy we bring to each encounter with them.

When Faith was in the womb, a geneticist saw genetic markers on a routine ultrasound and told my wife and me that Faith had a "fatal fetal anomaly" and that she was "incompatible with life." The doctor wanted my wife, Jesi,

---

Brad and Jesi Smith are married with five children. Brad works for Right to Life of Michigan, raising funds to defend the most vulnerable in our society. Brad and Jesi are speakers for SaveThe1.com, standing for all of those who are labeled as exceptions. They have spoken at numerous events for right-to-life groups, crisis pregnancy centers, and churches. They also actively help parents with disabled children to connect with doctors who support the lives of these precious children. You can reach them at bradjesi@proton.me for more information or for advocacy advice.

[1] Although similar to Down syndrome (also called Trisomy 21 because of an extra chromosome in the twenty-first pair), Trisomy 18 is a much harsher diagnosis than Down syndrome.

to have an amniocentesis done to confirm the diagnosis. Knowing this test could possibly cause a miscarriage, we declined in order to spare our already fragile daughter yet another obstacle. The intense pressure to get the amniocentesis led us to ask the question, "If we have the test done and you find a problem, can you help our daughter?" When the doctor replied no, the natural response was to question the purpose of the test. The doctor said, "To terminate." We both spontaneously responded, "That is not an option!" Our daughter was already loved and wanted—with or without disabilities. The geneticist kept trying to influence us by saying Faith would not live to her first birthday, and that even if she did live, her disability would ruin our finances and our marriage and negatively impact our four older children. The appointment ended abruptly, and we never went back.

The geneticist was right in his area of expertise. Through the ultrasound he correctly diagnosed Trisomy 18, but he stepped out of his area of expertise and training and his prognosis was wrong. This pernicious attitude is representative of a common view in the medical profession. Doctors often soften it by calling it "implicit bias". In reality, though, this bias is founded on the basic belief that a child's life is not worth living simply because she has a disability. It is discrimination and bigotry aimed at children with disabilities.

Faith was born on December 23, and by Christmas day the concerned neonatologist had called for a cardiologist to examine her. The cardiologist noted that she had a gigantic hole in her heart, known as a ventricular septal defect (VSD), and that surgery could repair it. He said "If you had to have heart surgery, this is the kind you would want to have, because it is 'one and done.' Once we fix it, we won't have to do anything else."

Two weeks later, with the diagnosis of Trisomy 18 confirmed, we met again with the cardiologist. He walked into the room with a stack of freshly printed papers still warm from the printer. He began to talk to us about the Trisomy 18 diagnosis and said these children do not do well with heart surgery because they are ten times more likely to die. (What he did not tell us was that 90 percent of Trisomy 18 children survive this type of heart surgery while 99 percent of typical children do.) Next he predicted that Faith would go into heart failure and that her lungs would fill with fluid. His remarks seemed intended to discourage us from taking any action. He then said he might be willing to do heart surgery if we still wanted it, but we would have to go before an ethics committee to get permission. Offended and appalled that we would have to justify our daughter's humanity and worth in order to get surgery, we left and never went back.

Doctors have done a lot for Faith, who had many serious medical challenges from the start. But we were mistaken in thinking she would receive the same level of care that other children automatically receive. She had a gastric tube inserted to ensure adequate nutrition, and later her tonsils as well as her adenoids were removed. Among many other procedures, she did eventually receive open-heart surgery to close the hole in her heart, and she also had a spinal fusion, a BiPap to open an obstructive airway—which was denied by the first hospital, nearly costing Faith's life—and jaw distraction surgery.

Our grave concern over her continual sickness and breathing difficulties led us to talk with Senator Rick Santorum, whose daughter Bella also has Trisomy 18. We learned from the discussion that Faith was not being offered the right treatment and care she needed. Senator Santorum worried that her breathing problem might stem from sleep apnea, something no doctor had even mentioned to us. We were skeptical of his advice at first, but we were desperate for any suggestions and help. As it turns out, he was correct, and the problem was remedied with a BiPap ventilator, which uses pressurized air with each breath to keep an obstructed airway open.

Senator Santorum also provided a list of items that would have been of great help to Faith—if the doctors at the hospital would have been willing to provide them. After her health issues escalated and Faith nearly died, we realized that they were simply not going to give her the care she needed. While our instinct was to trust in the medical professionals, we learned that such trust must be earned. In fact, when asking for certain treatments, one of the doctors told us, "No one does that for children like Faith." We had to leave that hospital system just to get routine care for a child they deemed unworthy.

This is also when we learned that there is such a thing as a "slow code," which means that medical providers offer the appearance of treatment, but purposely administer it so slowly that it is useless to the patient. The term is actually found in medical journals and involves a subtle form of deceit in the form of lethal neglect. One article in the *Journal of Perinatology* justified the methodology as a solution to infants with poor medical prognoses. We then understood why we had to push for Faith's sleep apnea to be addressed properly and for her to receive the device to allow her to breathe at night.

With all of these procedures, Faith has become healthier, stronger, and able to accomplish more in her life. After the jaw distraction surgery, at the age of two she took her first steps with the help of a gait trainer. This child who was never supposed to live, much less walk, did learn to walk, and thirteen years later, Faith has proven every dire prediction wrong. She loves her life, our marriage has been strengthened, and our four older children are wonderful, compassionate individuals, much in part because of their relationship with Faith.

Although Faith and many disabled individuals like her experience life differently than others, their intrinsic worth as human beings is self-evident. In fact, Faith enjoys her life and is happier than most of the people we know. When doctors refuse to treat their most challenging patients, everyone is diminished: the doctors lose opportunities to develop their medical skills and share knowledge about difficult cases, and they don't develop standards of care that help everyone. Conversely, the courageous doctors who treated Faith in situations where no standard of care existed have contributed to the medical profession and improved the practice of medicine for all patients.

Targeting vulnerable newborns and children with tests, policies, and laws is nothing new. During World War II, the Nazi regime implemented grotesque programs that turned some hospitals into killing wards, eliminating those who were deemed "useless eaters" and considered "life unworthy of life". Unwanted, mentally compromised, and disabled infants and children were euthanized. This was the first Nazi eugenics program, implemented almost two years before their other mass murder schemes. Facilities camouflaged such programs under the guise of offering the latest advanced treatments. In the present day, our country's practice of pushing abortion—under the guise of health care—as the solution to unwanted or disabled children, and offering compromised standards of healthcare to special-needs children, operates on the very same principle.

We experienced both the heavy-handed pressure from the medical community to abort our daughter, and their more subtle discouragement of life-saving care after her birth. Given no hope or help, many parents in similar situations are overwhelmed and easily deceived into thinking their child is better off dead, leading to the destruction of over 90 percent of such children. Despite the tremendous advances in the medical field to help the chronically ill, prenatal tests have become search-and-destroy missions for disabled children. To help fight this trend, my wife and I regularly help other families of special-needs babies, offering support and advice while connecting them with doctors who can provide proper care. In these raw, challenging encounters, we remember so well our own initial distress, mirrored in the "deer in the headlights" look we see in their eyes. The trauma of a difficult diagnosis can be devastating, and we want them to know that they need not feel helpless.

Faith has brought the best out of the people in her life, starting with us. Because of her, we are better parents and much more compassionate people. Her siblings understand a level of kindness and caring that most adults have not achieved. Her doctors and nurses have been challenged by her and have become more skilled in treating their patients. In fact, her ENT specialist has become one of the nation's premier experts for Trisomy 18 children through his willingness to care for and treat these children. Death does not need any help. It will come on its own without any prodding. Life takes work and at times even a struggle to be sustained. Faith and other children with disabilities are not only worth the battle, but they also lead the charge in renewing our nation's authentic compassion toward its children—and all others in need.

Now, you may read this and think that God gave us Faith

because we were capable and were already the perfect family for her. This has been expressed to us many times, but let me dispel this notion because we were completely overwhelmed. As parents, we were fearful about the future when we learned of Faith's diagnosis. There is nothing special about us. We simply loved our daughter.

It is often said that God will never give you more than you can handle. Let me tell you: He does, and He will intentionally give you more than you can handle so you drop to your knees and seek Him for help. This is a walk of faith in many ways. God has used the trials and tribulations of this journey to keep us humble before Him. We have grown under the load, and now, we are able to reassure other parents that He will do the same for them. The great blessing is that we get to see this take place repeatedly in other families —as the Lord meets them where they are, broken and disheartened, and turns them into warriors who fight through to victory. Oh, how we truly understand now that verse in Philippians, "I can do all things in [Christ] who strengthens me" (4:13).

Darlene Pawlik

It was 1966. In a small town in northern Massachusetts, Claire, a naïve schoolgirl, looked over her shoulder at half a dozen girls who were giggling and nearly swooning over what appeared to be a boy with a car. Claire was not nearly as impressed as the other girls. She was the eldest of four and had far too many responsibilities to be hovering around a novelty.

She rolled her eyes, shook her head slightly, shifted the weight of her books, and headed home. Claire was a frail girl from a poor family. Her fine, thin hair swirled in the breeze. She had brilliant green eyes that seemed to reflect the early spring foliage. The boy with the car, whose name was Dicky, took notice and followed her. He offered her a ride. She declined.

Claire's inattention to him only piqued his interest. He began to intercept her at school. Finally, Claire gave in. She accepted an invitation to go to a movie.

Darlene Pawlik is a native New Englander. She was conceived from rape when her mother was fifteen years old, then sexually abused and eventually sold into sex trafficking at fourteen. She became pregnant at the age of eighteen, as a result of life long sexual abuse. When her buyer threatened to kill her if she didn't have an abortion, pro-lifers provided a way of escape from her situation. She tells audiences that saving her baby saved her life. She has led the political action committee for New Hampshire Right to Life, served as vice president of the international organization Save the 1, and worked with the New Hampshire Traffick-Free Coalition and the New Hampshire Human Trafficking Collaborative Task Force. Darlene, who has five children and five grandchildren, resides in New Hampshire with her husband. For more information, visit TheDarlingPrincess.com.

That afternoon, Dicky picked her up in his car. They drove to the theater and watched the movie, enjoying plenty of popcorn and soda. One the way back, he took a shortcut. It was dark and raining. Claire was anxious to get home. She had chores and some homework to do, but Dicky had other plans. He pulled into a sandpit and forced himself on her.

She tried to get free. Grasping at everything. She couldn't fight him off. Ashamed and humiliated, she curled up in a ball as he drove, until he pulled up in front of her house.

As she walked toward the house, she could see her father through the window, and she knew her mom was at work. She pushed the wet hair from her face and, to avoid being seen, sneaked up the stairs. As she fell onto her bed, tears streamed down her face. In silence, she hoped no one would ever know.

When she returned to school, she couldn't avoid him. He approached her in plain view of other students.

He apologized for being rough and said, "You turned me on."

Claire closed her eyes and turned away, the pain on her face plainly visible to anyone who cared to look. He circled in front of her. She recoiled and backed away.

Within a few weeks, Claire realized she was pregnant. Dicky said he was sorry and that he'd change. He was so convincing. So she married him. During their marriage, he continued to attack her suddenly and violently.

Pregnant a second time and on the verge of suicide from the perpetual abuse, Claire realized she needed to confide in someone. She told her mother about everything that had happened and asked for help. How glad I am that she did because Claire is my mother.

Even though people were aware of Dicky's abuses, my baby sister and I were sent to visit our paternal grandmother, where he had access to us. Tricky Dicky, as he was known, was allowed to take many women and children into the barn on her property, there doing whatever he pleased with absolute impunity.

We were taught to be silent, to keep secrets. Subtle enticements and numerous threats ensured compliance.

One of my earliest memories was of my paternal grandmother taking me into her room, in which boxes were stacked from floor to ceiling. She reached into a box and pulled out a little dress, some black patent leather shoes, and frilly socks. She dressed me. Then, she brought me out and placed me in her son's arms like a wrapped gift. He carried me down the flagstone path to the barn. I can still hear the sand crunching under his feet.

My mom married again, and her second husband legally adopted us. I was glad to have a new name. He took us to a little Congregational church down the road from his parents. His mother was exceedingly kind, and she gave me my first Bible. After his father got sick, we lived with them for a while. It was so different from being at my paternal grandmother's. We played with cousins next door and picked berries at a nearby farm. It was a peaceful place.

Unfortunately, the second marriage also ended in divorce, and we moved to a rundown, three-story tenement in a nearby mill city. My mother had to work and was also attending school, hoping for a better job. She rented a room to her brother to help pay the bills.

One night, in a drunken state, her brother molested me. All the rage from the previous incidents of abuse rose to the surface, and I turned to drugs and alcohol to try to numb the intense pain of a marred identity—to no avail. Masking the pain only intensified it. My world spun out of control. I skipped school, sneaked out at night, and stole money from my mother for drugs. I kicked the windows out of the old-fashioned bus stop shelter and scattered trash in the streets. I had no respect, no hope, and no vision for the future.

I was that notorious kid, the one you wouldn't let your kids be around. A gruff, crass exterior hid a deeply wounded little girl. I was about ninety pounds and five feet tall, with a child's build, thick blond hair, and very blue eyes. Crooked teeth, too big for my mouth, made me cautious about smiling, so I reserved my smile for rare occasions. If I let my guard down, someone was sure to point out that I needed braces.

I felt like I had a mark on my forehead that attracted abusers and gave them some weird permission to take advantage of me or treat me badly. I had no words for that feeling, but surely felt unworthy of love and respect. My entire existence seemed to be determined by outside forces. It was as if I had no control and was floating downstream, in a life I didn't own.

I remember 1980 as a wild year. My uncle was still at the apartment, drinking excessively with outbursts of vulgarity and violence, which brought the police at times. My maternal grandmother and her friend also stayed at the apartment, adding to the chaos. They drank. We all drank. And Valium was introduced.

I had been the quiet one, but not anymore. I was totally out of control, often leaving school after the free breakfast to drink beer and smoke pot all day, watch TV or play cards. When confronted, I would fly into a rage, screaming and throwing furniture around. My mom filed a request with our county's intervention agency and we met with counselors and social workers, but it wasn't what I needed. What I needed was a safe place to process my trauma.

The spring when I was thirteen, Ace started hanging

around the neighborhood. He was a bodybuilder from the YMCA who drove a black Lincoln Continental with a red leather interior. That car shined! He wouldn't let anyone touch it. He had jet-black hair and dark brown eyes, a great big smile, and always smelled good. He was friendly with all the kids on my block.

It never occurred to me to question why he wasn't at work, but instead driving around and hanging out in neighborhoods with kids. I didn't know I was his target, that he had a queue of girls in various stages of grooming, and that he sold girls like me to men for sex. I knew nothing.

Ace drove up beside me one morning, "What are you doing out in the cold?" he asked.

"Nothing," I said.

"Jump in," he offered.

He took me to his apartment to have sex with him. It was casual and friendly, not romantic. It wasn't pressured either. He spent months, gradually talking to me about the things I needed or wanted, sometimes implying I could get things by having sex with others. I declined.

"You can have the things you want, the things you need," he persisted.

I declined until, on my fourteenth birthday, my mom came home from running errands. I stood across the table and reminded her, sarcastically, of the glorious day. Walking past me, she said, "Here" as she took two crumpled dollars from her purse and put them on the table as my birthday gift.

I was devastated. I wasn't thinking of all the trouble I'd caused by stealing her money, throwing furniture, fighting with the neighbors, drinking, smoking pot, skipping school, and all sorts of embarrassments. But the rejection was too much. I called Ace. He sold me that day to a businessman from Atkinson, New Hampshire who was thrilled that I was so young and awkward. Ace sold me hundreds of more times—in alleyways, in his car—always profiting from the damage done to my body and soul. His clients ranged from drunken, violent creeps to a city councilman, a doctor, and other professionals, most of whom were old white men.

When I was seventeen, I was sold to one of my early buyers as a "house pet." Having by then been passed around for years without becoming pregnant, I assumed it wouldn't happen. But after feeling weak and faint for days, I went to the emergency room, where to my shock I found that I was pregnant. The nurse immediately set up an appointment at Planned Parenthood, but I didn't want to go. My buyer had been abundantly clear about his expectations and bragged that the previous women he used had been forced to abort. So when I returned home, I threw myself at his feet and begged him to just let me leave him to have the child. He said that if I didn't have the abortion, he would kill me.

After he left, I cried myself to sleep. In a dream of the abortion procedure, in color, from the perspective of inside the womb, I saw body parts. Terrified, I jumped out of bed, threw my hands in the air, and said, "God, if You're real, I need You to show up." Then, I remembered one special social worker, Anthy, who had tracked me as a runaway. She was kind when she really didn't need to be, and she never gave up on me.

I called Anthy and she found a place for me in a home for unwed mothers. Knowing I had a safe place to go to, I had dinner with the baby's father that evening and convinced him that I had gone through with the abortion. Then I fled, never to see him again.

I had my baby, thanks to the Friends of the Unborn maternity shelter. A woman named Marilyn opened her home to us and took us on retreats where we learned how to pray, and they taught us strategies to help us process the trauma we'd been through. This was the beginning of my healing process, but it would take a long time to grasp the depth of damage wrought in those early years. I came to the realization that my self-destructive behaviors were simply the manifestation of my inner turmoil.

It wasn't until I began nursing school that I began to see the fidelity of God. One teacher, remembering me as a child, showed me a photo of his Sunday school class, and there I was in the front row. He said that I had professed Christ as my Savior while there—around the age of ten. All these years later I was struck by the profound meaning of that simple profession and God's response.

After graduating from nursing school, I had another child; then I got married and had three more. Healing from all the trauma and grief was arduous and slow, and my husband and children suffered greatly from my mistakes. Part of the messiness of life is that sin is never just personal, but God's grace and mercy bring healing to those who seek Him.

My story is just one of millions of similar tales: abused girls becoming trapped in a continuing cycle of abuse, leading to forced abortions and compounded devastation. When free will is abused and choices are made to destroy rather than to create, our God-given identities become obscured. For the perpetrators as well as the victims, the damaging effects run deep.

One thread that runs through my life is that, like my mom, I was given the grace to recognize the tiny, unseen beings within the womb as persons worth protecting. "We were in it together," she said when she told me the story of my conception. That life-saving message stuck with me, and where there's life, there's hope.

Dr. Dermot Kearney

On a Saturday night in mid-January 2021, I heard the telltale signal of a new WhatsApp message on my mobile phone. It was a request from a nurse working with Heartbeat International, an Ohio-based pro-life organization. Linda (not her real name), a young woman in the north of England, needed urgent help. She had taken mifepristone, a chemical abortion pill, seven hours earlier. Now she regretted it and was desperate to save her baby. An ultrasound scan performed two days earlier revealed she was five weeks and two days pregnant.

Linda had already done some research and was aware that progesterone, if administered promptly, might preserve her pregnancy by blocking the ongoing effects of mifepristone. Following a detailed consultation, she agreed to travel to a pharmacy that could dispense to her an oral progesterone (Utrogestan). There was, however, a problem. It was almost 11:30 P.M., and the only pharmacy still open for business in her area was in another town almost thirty miles away. I called that pharmacy and fortunately they had progesterone in stock and were satisfied to accept an e-mail prescription. The pharmacist commented, however, that the patient might

---

Dermot Kearney is a consultant cardiologist and current president of the Catholic Medical Association (UK). He obtained a medical degree from University College Dublin, Ireland, in 1989. Following general medical and cardiology specialist training in Ireland, Dr. Kearney completed a fellowship in interventional cardiology in Leiden and Amsterdam, Netherlands. Since 2003, he has held a cardiology post at Queen Elizabeth Hospital, Gateshead.

not arrive in time, since the store would be closing at midnight.

Linda and her partner were determined to save the baby, and to start progesterone rescue treatment as soon as possible. If she could not obtain progesterone that night, she would have to wait at least another twelve hours, and she knew that such a delay could greatly increase the risk of her baby not surviving.

In desperation, she called the pharmacy during the thirty-mile car journey with her partner. She pleaded with the sympathetic pharmacist on duty to keep the store open for an extra fifteen minutes, since her baby's life might depend upon it. The pharmacist did what she asked, and Linda was able to start rescue treatment that night.

Eight months later, in September 2021, Linda gave birth to a healthy baby girl.

This encounter with Linda was the forty-fourth abortion pill reversal (APR) consultation that I had undertaken since my first such experience in June 2020. I would go on to have ninety-two of these consultations, until ordered to discontinue the service by the UK medical regulatory authorities in April 2021.

Most abortions are now conducted by medical or pharmacological means rather than surgery. In the UK in 2020, 85 percent of more than 220,000 abortions were chemically induced via a two-stage drug administration process. The first abortion pill, mifepristone, is taken to block the action of natural progesterone, which is essential to maintaining pregnancy. A second drug, misoprostol, a prostaglandin analogue, is taken twenty-four to forty-eight hours later to complete the abortion process by inducing strong uterine contractions. When both drugs are taken, there is a 98 to 99 percent certainty that the baby will be killed. If the mother takes the first abortion pill and decides not to take the second pill, but doesn't receive any progesterone rescue therapy, there is a 20 to 25 percent chance that her baby will survive. If she doesn't take the follow-up misoprostol and receives rescue treatment promptly with progesterone therapy, the chance of her baby surviving is greatly enhanced, with survival rates of 50 to 70 percent.

The chance of fetal survival is influenced by a number of factors, including the age of gestation when mifepristone was taken, the duration of time between mifepristone ingestion and commencing rescue treatment with progesterone, and the general health of the mother and her previous obstetric history. The method of progesterone administration and possibly other currently unknown factors may also play important roles in determining the outcome.

In the United States, an abortion pill reversal (APR) program using progesterone had been established in 2012; I became aware of it in 2014. I am a member of the United Kingdom's branch of the Catholic Medical Association (CMA) and that year our Council was approached by Jack Scarisbrick, the founder of Life, a UK-based pro-life organization. He asked if we could help women who regretted having taken the first abortion pill and were in need of advice about how to save their babies. Initially we were skeptical that such a treatment could be effective. We were also concerned about possible safety aspects, for both mother and child, if pregnancy continued after exposure to the abortion drugs. Despite our reservations, however, we agreed to investigate the issue.

Not much information was available in 2014. A handful of academic articles had been published. We noted that there was already considerable opposition to APR in the United States. I read all the arguments from both sides of the debate.

Over time, evidence emerged that favorably demonstrated the efficacy and safety of APR.

An important turning point for me was a *New York Times Magazine* article in July 2017 titled "A New Front in the War over Reproductive Rights: Abortion Pill Reversal." It was a well-balanced account with opinions from those on both sides. I was particularly impressed by a statement from Harvey Kliman, a professor of placental research at the Yale School of Medicine. He believed that APR made "biological sense." He proclaimed that if his daughter had accidentally taken mifepristone while pregnant, he would recommend progesterone treatments to save the baby. He added, "I bet you it would work." What was most convincing was that Professor Kliman, who was described as being pro-choice, was obviously an authority on this question.

In May 2018, Clare McCullough from Good Counsel Network, another pro-life organization, pleaded with the CMA to help the many women who were seeking to save their babies after having taken the first abortion pill. As the newly elected president of the CMA, I reassured Clare that we would respond to this call for help.

I continued to research the issue and attended the CMA's annual educational conference in Dallas in October 2018. There I had the opportunity to meet APR pioneers and leading experts, including Dr. George Delgado, who gave a presentation titled "Abortion Pill Reversal: Offering Women a Second Chance." I was convinced that an APR program was necessary in the UK and that it should be possible to establish one, but at that time I had no idea how that could be achieved.

Following further CMA Council discussions, letters were written to the Royal College of Obstetricians & Gynaecologists (RCOG), the Royal College of General Practitioners

(RCGP), and National Health Service England (NHSE), informing them about APR. We requested that efforts be made to establish APR as a mainstream medical service in the UK, since increasing numbers of women were seeking help. We also noted that the evidence from the United States regarding the safety and efficacy of APR using progesterone was very convincing.

The delayed responses we received were predictably disappointing and unsupportive. It was particularly puzzling that both the RCOG and RCGP leadership stated that they would not support the use of a medical product unlicensed for use in APR. They failed to acknowledge that misoprostol, the second abortion drug, is not licensed for use in abortion. It is licensed for use in the management of peptic ulcer disease. We highlighted this inconsistency and also pointed out that the RCOG recommended the use of methotrexate in treating ectopic pregnancies, even though this drug is not licensed for such use. It is licensed for use in the management of chronic inflammatory conditions such as rheumatoid arthritis. We received no response to these second letters.

The response from NHSE was also quite pathetic. We were informed that NHSE could not support APR because there was no evidence base for its use, and "expectant management" should be advised in the event of a woman changing her mind after taking mifepristone. Expectant management simply means waiting to see what might happen without any active intervention. Bear in mind, we had demonstrated evidence of a significant improvement in survival when APR was employed compared to expectant management alone. This evidence was ignored.

The CMA Council then contacted the General Medical Council (GMC), posing a simple question. We asked how a doctor should respond if a woman regrets her decision after taking mifepristone. In effect, we were seeking guidance on how a doctor should respond to a pregnant woman who has withdrawn her consent partway through a medical abortion process. The GMC responded that it could not comment on specific clinical questions, but reminded us that every patient has a right to be informed of all treatment options available at every stage, and to withdraw consent at any point in relation to any treatment.

While the GMC did not definitively support the use of APR, it certainly didn't warn that APR must not be offered to women seeking to save their babies after taking mifepristone. Final letters were then written to the RCOG, RCGP, and NHSE executives, quoting the GMC response. Each letter ended with the statement that we presumed there would be no objections at that stage if the general public were made aware of APR. No responses were received.

The main stumbling block to establishing an effective APR service was finding a way for women seeking help to gain quick access to a doctor willing to provide it. This problem was overcome almost by accident in April 2020.

Heartbeat International, which operates the Abortion Pill Rescue Network, received a call from a woman in the UK seeking immediate help after having taken mifepristone earlier that day. She had contacted the abortion clinic that had provided the abortion pills for her but was told that nothing could be done. In desperation, she undertook an internet search for abortion reversal and found the Heartbeat help line.

At that time, no doctors in the UK were registered with the help line, so a doctor in the Republic of Ireland was contacted. Because he was unable to prescribe medications in the UK, he contacted Dr. Eileen Reilly, a UK-based obstetrician-gynecologist. She was able to help the prospective mother by prescribed progesterone via e-mail once she located a pharmacy willing to dispense the medication immediately.

Knowing of my interest in establishing an APR service in the UK, Dr. Reilly informed me of her experience and her belief that registering with Heartbeat International could be a real game-changer. That proved to be the case. I received my first request for APR in late June 2020.

Initially, requests for help were occasional—about one every two to three weeks. By September 2020, however, the number of requests increased week by week. Some days, especially at weekends, I was receiving up to three requests a day, and most weeks brought six or seven personal consultations, not to mention those provided by Dr. Reilly. Eventually we were both on duty, available for consultations twenty-four hours a day, seven days a week.

By late April 2021, I had received ninety-two calls for help, and Dr. Reilly had dealt with fifty-two. Then in mid-February 2021, both Heartbeat International and Dr. Reilly were victims of a fake request from a person who describes herself as an "investigative journalist". The "journalist" subsequently wrote a scathing article attacking APR and doctors providing the service, even though Dr. Reilly had handled the "consultation" in a sympathetic and professional manner. We did not realize at that stage that a more extensive and orchestrated attack on APR and doctors providing it in the UK was already well underway.

Of the 144 women who requested help, 91 commenced progesterone rescue treatment. There are myriad reasons why the others did not commence APR, mostly related to coercion to continue with the abortion, but sometimes because they had already experienced heavy bleeding and severe abdominal cramps, suggesting that rescue treatment might be too late.

Of the 91 who commenced APR, 67 completed the treatment, and 16 did not; 8 patients could not be located for follow-up. Of the 67 mothers who followed through with the treatment, 32 successfully delivered healthy babies. This represents an overall success rate of 48 percent.

Our APR service in the UK came to an abrupt halt on April 28, 2021. Both Dr. Reilly and I received notification from the GMC of complaints about our APR work from a variety of sources. We were told we were under investigation for the possibility of serious professional misconduct and were each ordered to attend separate Interim Order Tribunal (IOT) hearings on May 12, 2021.

The sources of complaint were revealed as Marie Stopes International (an abortion provider now known as MSI Reproductive Choices in an attempt to hide the identity of its racist eugenicist founder), the RCOG, and the pro-abortion advocacy group Open Democracy. No complaints came from any of the mothers we had cared for or from their families.

There were ten specific allegations against me, including that I had inappropriately and remotely prescribed an unlicensed medication, with no evidence base and outside of valid clinical guidelines, and that I had made no attempt to discuss a patient's care with MSI's clinical team. Additionally, it was claimed that I had made a patient feel "in debt" to me by offering to pay for scans and by offering to help with childcare. I was also charged with denying her an opportunity to be referred for independent counseling to help her decision making. In doing so, it was alleged that I had imposed my anti-abortion personal beliefs, without any attempt to present an impartial, evidence-based approach to her care.

It was further alleged that I had offered to arrange for ultrasound scans to be carried out privately, and that such private scans might fail to screen for fetal abnormalities. Thus it was claimed that I had caused a patient distress by preventing her from making an informed choice about her pregnancy options.

Perhaps the most nonsensical charge of all was that I had failed to follow National Institute of Clinical Care Excellence (NICE) guidelines for abortion care, and that I had repeatedly acted outside of my area of competence. There were also allegations that I had failed to obtain "consent" from patients and to keep suitable medical records.

It was extremely disappointing that the GMC, the sole regulatory body for doctors practicing medicine in the UK, endorsed all these allegations without a single item of evidence to support them, and that they presented them in full at the initial IOT hearing on May 12 purely on the basis of hearsay from the abortion industry.

The GMC legal representative was particularly vindictive when he stated that I had been disingenuous in my written response to these allegations. I had described how I had previously written to the GMC in 2019 seeking guidance and I quoted directly from the response received. I had also mentioned that I, as president of the CMA, had represented the Association on the GMC's own strategic forum on equality, diversity, and inclusion and that, at an April 2021 meeting, I had delivered a full report on the involvement of CMA members in providing the APR service to women in the UK

No apology has been received from the GMC regarding the endorsement of these accusations, which were later proven to be unfounded. It is appalling that the GMC allowed itself to be manipulated by the abortion industry to pursue an ideological and political agenda.

Of particular concern was the GMC endorsement of a complaint from the RCOG expressing anti-Catholic sentiments. In their letter, the RCOG stated that its main concern was not so much the APR treatment that had been provided, but rather the "people providing this service." They highlighted the fact that one of these doctors was the president of the Catholic Medical Association, implying that vulnerable women seeking help would therefore not receive appropriate care.

At both IOT hearings, the GMC requested that, due to the seriousness of the allegations, the doctors providing the APR service should be suspended from all medical practice for the maximum period of eighteen months. They asserted that such professional misconduct represented a danger to the public. The IOT considered the allegations but did not look at any factual evidence. The chair of the Tribunal repeatedly stated that the hearing was not a "fact-finding" exercise and that the "veracity" of the allegations would not be examined. Dr. Reilly and I both received the same penalty with "conditions" imposed upon our licenses to practice medicine in the UK In my case, the main condition was that I "must not prescribe, administer, or recommend progesterone for abortion reversal treatments." I was also banned from carrying out any voluntary or private work as a medical doctor without the expressed permission of the GMC. I thus probably became the first doctor in the history of medicine to be banned from saving lives.

As an ob/gyn, Dr. Reilly was allowed to continue prescribing progesterone, but was forbidden to carry out any medical activities without supervision and without permission from the GMC. We were both allowed to continue our normal NHS-contracted work, at least for the moment, pending an investigation. These conditions were imposed for an eighteen-month period but were to be reviewed every six months. A later hearing could result in our removal from the medical register and disqualification from medical practice within the UK

When the initial allegations were made known, the UK-based charity Christian Concern/Christian Legal Centre immediately stepped in. They offered pro bono legal assistance to both of us, and plans were put in place to fight the injustice. Dr. Reilly opted for a different secular legal representation. In preparation for that first IOT, an independent expert witness report had been obtained but wasn't even considered at the hearing. Following the IOT, steps were immediately taken to obtain witness statements from a number of the mothers who had sought APR treatment. We knew that our strongest defense would be supportive statements from these women.

We obtained ten such statements but could have easily obtained many more if more had been required. The stories were all different. Some came from mothers who had received APR treatment and had already given birth to happy, healthy babies. Others came from mothers who were still in various stages of pregnancy. Two statements came from mothers who had suffered miscarriages after taking mifepristone, despite receiving APR therapy. There were also two statements from mothers who had decided to proceed with abortion by taking the second abortion pill, misoprostol, and not opting for progesterone rescue treatment. One of them had contacted me a number of days later to express her gratitude that a doctor had taken the time to honestly explain to her the whole process of abortion induced by pills, and the counteractive APR treatment. She was grateful that options other than abortion had been presented to her. She deeply regretted that she had not accepted the APR offer and was resigned to accepting that she had to live with her terrible mistake. It was an opportunity to provide consolation to her and to assist with her healing process. We have kept in touch and she is making a good recovery following the trauma of abortion that she felt pressured to undergo.

The comments from these courageous ladies were very moving:

"We love him so much. He is perfect. If not for you, we wouldn't have him. Thank you so much! Can't express how grateful we are for everything you have done for us."

"I will be eternally grateful for your help. I'll always carry the guilt, but this has been a miracle in itself."

"I just want to thank you for all the help and support you have given me. I am truly grateful."

"You have helped me so much. I cannot thank you enough."

"Your kindness will never be forgotten and the help you gave us gave our baby a chance. Thank you from the bottom of my heart. If anything, my faith in humanity was restored."

"I'm loving your support. It's really helped me get through this. I feel incredibly lucky to be given this hope and aid."

"Thank you, Dermot. Oh, I so hope this all works out and you are seen for the incredible doctor you really are. Not many would go above and beyond like you do."

"Thank you so much. I don't have any right to decide anyone's life and every baby deserves a life. I am so grateful that we were given a second chance. I can't wait to go for a scan."

"Please feel free to share [photo of newborn baby boy] with your APR team. Maybe his photos could give another woman or family hope. Just like your entire team gave mine."

"We are so grateful for all your help and know we might not have had our little one if it wasn't for everything you did . . . makes me well up a bit thinking of not having her and how close we were."

"Thank you so much for all your help. You've no idea how much it means."

"I thought my baby won't survive but I'm currently at twenty-one weeks and I'm pleased to say I'm having a healthy baby girl. She's measuring absolutely perfect. She has the strongest heartbeat and she's fighting, and I really couldn't thank Dermot more. He saved my daughter's life from abortion I never ever wanted. He's doing an amazing job and he's very, very supportive. He's been there the whole way through my journey. He's the most kind-hearted man you could ever work alongside."

"I really appreciate everything you've done . . . I don't think It would have been as easy without you. . . . You have been super. Your clients are very lucky."

Following an appeal, I was granted an early review with a further tribunal hearing on August 3, 2021. I had been informed that the reason for this appeal was the emergence of new evidence, namely the witness statements we had provided. No evidence had yet been produced by the GMC to support the allegations against me. The medical director of MSI Reproductive Choices had harassed one of the mothers who had written a strongly supportive statement in my favor, and he had tried to persuade her to make false statements about me and my role in providing progesterone treatment for her. She had informed MSI that she was considering APR with progesterone after she regretted taking mifepristone. She was apparently persuaded by MSI that APR was ineffective and that she should complete the abortion process. She followed that advice but regretted it after suffering the induced miscarriage. She experienced significant post-abortive complications as she had an incomplete abortion and developed an intra-uterine infection that required antibiotic therapy and surgery to complete uterine evacuation. The medical director of MSI had tried to convince her that these complications were related to my involvement in her case, even though she had not taken the progesterone tablets.

We know, from Freedom of Information access to NHS medical records, that a large number of women (at least 1 in 17), suffer serious complications from chemically induced abortions. Each month, an average of 495 women in the UK require emergency care assessments as a result of abortion-related complications. The vast majority of the cases arise from incomplete abortions and subsequent risks of serious infections and severe hemorrhaging. The complication rate is four times that associated with surgical abortion. The evidence concerning the attempt by the MSI medical director to persuade a witness to make false accusations was presented to the IOT.

My legal team from Christian Legal Centre and I were dismayed when the chair of the IOT review announced at the start that, once again, it was not a "fact-finding" hearing and the "veracity" of any evidence produced would not be determined. This was very disappointing and essentially turned the hearing into a farce with the outcome already decided. It was not surprising that the conditions imposed at my first hearing in May 2021 remained in place after this "early review."

Unperturbed, my legal team was determined to ensure that all of the evidence obtained would be brought before a proper judicial system. We decided to take our case to the High Court. Our appeal to the High Court was based on the premise that the actual evidence failed to demonstrate any real risk of impairment of fitness to practice, that it failed to demonstrate that the conditions imposed were necessary for the protection of the public, and that the Interim Order was not proportionate. A High Court hearing was subsequently arranged for Thursday, February 24, 2022.

The GMC had still not managed to find any independent expert witness to provide a report by the time of the High Court notification, even though many months had elapsed since the initial IOT hearing. They had confirmed, on several occasions, that they were having difficulty in finding an expert witness to assess the case. A report was eventually received on February 11, 2022. It was largely supportive of APR and the principles of the service. The expert declared there was no evidence of danger to the mother or to her developing fetus in providing APR. He accepted the existence of an evidence base to support the use of APR.

He expressed some concern about my offers to assist some of the mothers financially in paying for the progesterone treatment if they were unable to meet the cost themselves. Of note, however, he had not been allowed to see any of the witness statements from the mothers or from the other independent expert witness. His concern needed to be addressed, and we explained that the offer of financial assistance was made only after the mother had voluntarily given her fully informed consent to proceed with APR. We made it clear that the payment was for the medication only (essentially to the pharmacist dispensing the progesterone treatment) and was not a payment to the mother.

As we continued to prepare for the High Court appearance on February 24, we were informed that all of the evidence was passed to the GMC case examiners for assessment.

On the morning of Tuesday, February 15, 2022, I received a phone call from my lawyer informing me that the GMC had closed the case. Moments later, an e-mail from the GMC confirmed that "the case examiners have considered the information provided by MSI Reproductive Choices, Open Democracy, Safe Abortion Action Fund UK, and the Royal College of Obstetricians and Gynaecologists, and decided to conclude this case with no further action." In the final outcome report, the case examiners accepted that there was "no prospect" of finding any evidence to support any of the allegations that had been endorsed by the GMC against me.

The conditions imposed upon Dr. Reilly remained in place until her case was formally closed on March 28, 2022. Her legal team had not proposed any referral to the High Court.

In the nine-month period from May 2021 to the end of January 2022, 160 women in the UK contacted the Heartbeat International help line seeking help after taking mifepristone. Sadly, they were all informed that no doctor in the UK was available to support them because of restrictions imposed by the GMC.

Of those 160 women, it is likely that at least 100 of them would have commenced APR treatment had it been prescribed. At least 50 would have had continuing pregnancies. Hopefully some of them have managed to save their babies by not taking misoprostol, although they would not have received the continuing support that APR doctors provide. A conservative estimate suggests that at least 30 babies died who would otherwise have been saved if APR services had been available for these mothers.

I have given you an account of these matters so that you may know two important things: (1) the depths of deceit by the enemy and (2) that we can and will win this fight.

There is no greater argument against abortion than a living, breathing, smiling child who was saved from the clutches of the abortion industry. That is why they worked so hard to shut us down. But we have Almighty God on our side. Who can be against us?

Dr. Stephen D. Hammond

It was 1977. The young resident had just turned twenty-eight years old and had the world by the tail. With the difficult years of medical school behind him, he was halfway through his residency and well on the way to realizing his dream of becoming an obstetrician-gynecologist. As soon as he began his obstetrics rotation in medical school, he had decided to pursue this specialty. Delivering babies was so interesting to him—especially the final product: a squirming, slippery little boy or girl emitting that first important cry and melting hearts. This was a specialty that brought incredible happiness to people.

The long hours were only a minor annoyance at his age. Part of the excitement of youth is the ability to stay up all night! He was sure that this is what he wanted to do for the rest of his life. During his medical school obstetric rotation, as well as an internship, some moonlighting as an extern, and a year of residency, he had gained experience

---

Stephen Hammond has practiced obstetrics and gynecology in Jackson, Tennessee, for over forty years. He is certified by the American Board of Obstetricians and Gynecologists, a fellow of the American College of Obstetricians and Gynecologists, and the medical director of clinical research at the Jackson Clinic. He has served as the principal investigator for scores of clinical trials. Over the course of his career, he has delivered over four thousand babies. As a resident at the Medical College of Georgia, Hammond performed more than 700 abortions, but today he is a strong proponent of the pro-life movement, speaking to groups and students on the sanctity of life. With Emily LaBonte, he co-authored the book *The Christian and Abortion: A Nonnegotiable Stance* (Grand Rapids, Mich.: Credo House, 2019).

in both routine and complicated deliveries, including those where forceps or breech extractions were required. He had also learned to do Cesarean sections without the presence of a chief resident assistant and was competent to perform hysterectomies and other surgeries in the emerging field of laparoscopy.

Laparoscopy, which involves inserting an instrument into the abdomen through a very small incision, was first developed by gynecologists to perform tubal ligations. Today, laparoscopy is enhanced by the use of videos and special equipment that have made it possible to do even major surgeries with small incisions. But when the technology was in its infancy, there was great excitement over even its limited scope. During the student's residency, laparoscopy was taught by a physician who oversaw residency training at the Planned Parenthood facility. Then he was introduced to another procedure that had been legalized in the United States just four years earlier: abortion.

The landmark *Roe v. Wade* decision brought social and political changes, and the young resident saw no reason why he shouldn't be a part of this cutting-edge movement. The logic and arguments seemed clear and compelling to him: women now had access to legal and "safe" terminations of unwanted pregnancies. Moreover, the expertise to perform the procedure was part of the training with which any good ob-gyn needed to be familiar.

Competency with the "procedure" required developing some important skills, the first of which was the ability to determine the approximate gestational age of the fetus. This was accomplished by a bimanual (two-handed) exam in which one gloved hand is inserted into the vagina to push the uterus up out of the pelvis so the other hand could then palpate and determine the size of the uterus. This skill was important because real-time ultrasound, which can quickly determine the gestational age with great accuracy, was not available in 1977. Second, the resident had to become proficient in dilating the cervix, the narrow cylinder of firm connective tissue that opens into the womb. In the first trimester of a pregnancy the cervix is firmly closed, so one method of forcing it open is to insert a metal dilator that opens it wide enough for a plastic cannula, or tube, to be inserted. Alternatively, a dried form of compressed seaweed called laminaria can be inserted, which after a day will swell and expand with the moisture from the cervix, forcing an opening. Since the laminaria method requires two visits, which isn't always feasible, the former, more painful method is typically used, and a local anesthetic is injected around the cervix. This is called a paracervical block. This step requires some expertise because the cervix may be very tight, and forcing it open can cause lacerations or create a false channel, causing a perforation. After conducting a few hundred of these procedures, the resident felt comfortable that he could handle even the most difficult of cases.

The insertion of the plastic cannula also requires expertise. The cannula is just six to nine millimeters in diameter and is introduced through the cervix into the pregnant uterus. The pregnant uterus is soft and if care is not taken, the cannula can be pushed through the wall of the uterus, which can potentially cause major internal bleeding. In addition, if a perforation is not recognized, the cannula perforating the uterus is now inside the abdomen. When suction begins (which is the next step in the abortion process), a cannula inside the abdomen could damage the intestine, bladder, or other vital structures. Knowing how far to insert the cannula and how much pressure to exert on it is a learned skill, and the eager young doctor became proficient at this part of the procedure, too.

Once the suction tubing is connected to the cannula, the "aborting" begins. The opening on the end of the cannula is very small so it can't remove the fetus intact. The amniotic sac, which is the bag of water around the baby containing roughly a half a cup of fluid, has to first be ruptured. Thus the fluid flows clearly at first and then becomes bloody as the cannula suctions the placenta, membranes, and finally the fetus, which is torn into pieces and then vacuumed up. A six-to-eight-week fetus is only two to three centimeters long but even at that small size the "pieces" of the fetus are easily recognizable. A twelve-week fetus is around seven to ten centimeters long. At this stage it is even easier to recognize fetal parts for what they are: hands, legs, feet, torso, and head—with the eyes and mouth easily discernible. The doctors were trained to ignore the mothers' crying, and even their occasional pleas to stop, and usually at this stage the procedure was past the point of return.

The next step in the process was to collect the fetal body parts and make sure they were all accounted for, which is done out of view of the patient. The resident learned to dissect the baby parts with the cold clinical approach that a forensic pathologist would employ during an autopsy. No emotion. He became so good at this procedure that he was hired by Planned Parenthood to do abortions for them on Saturdays when he was not on call. These Saturday procedures were medically easier because the patients he attended had usually been given laminaria the day before, so neither bimanual exams nor metal dilations of the cervix were needed.

This went on for a year until something unexpected happened. A sixteen-year-old girl, who seemed more nervous than most of his clients, was the last patient that morning. He inserted the cannula just as he had done so many times before and the amniotic fluid began to fill the device. And it filled the device more and more. After a quart or more of fluid, he knew something was wrong. Then he felt it. The baby kicked him!

He had a one-year-old boy at home so he knew what a baby's kick felt like. Every time he changed his son's diaper, he experienced those powerful leg thrusts, and this felt just like that. The kicking continued—the baby was aggressively squirming inside the womb. He realized the girl had lied about her dates and the faculty member had missed the fact that she was at least twenty-two to twenty-four weeks pregnant. A feeling of dread swept over him. What was he going to do now? Eventually he arranged for the girl to be transferred to a hospital, where she was anesthetized and underwent a dilation and extraction (D&X) procedure. The baby had to be broken up into small pieces so that he could be removed. That was the last abortion the resident ever did.

I was that young resident.

I was in my second year of practicing medicine. Until then I had been convinced that abortion was just another procedure and that I was helping women. I believed that if my patient and I decided that the best thing for her was to end her pregnancy, then the government should not interfere. I was wrong. I was wrong seven hundred times.

The child is not the only victim of abortion. For many years I have listened to women share their painful memories and haunting questions that persist long after they walk out of Planned Parenthood.

Having been raised in a Christian home, my earliest memories are of my mother teaching me about God, sin, love, and heaven. I had a mature understanding of God as a child, sensing not only His ability to watch over me but His omnipresence. I could do nothing outside of His knowledge. As I struggled as a youngster to behave and to love others, I knew that Jesus was my hope, and that through the Cross He offered me both love and forgiveness.

So what happened? I went from being a young Christian to a physician well-trained in how to care for human beings, who subsequently turned his back on that responsibility, ending the lives of over seven hundred babies. I could blame the Church for not giving me the ammunition to resist the indoctrination I received in medical school. I could blame my parents for not saying: "We raised you better than that" (they didn't say a word against me being an abortionist). But the truth is that I can blame only myself. I should have been a better student of what the Bible says about the sanctity of human life and the pitfalls of worldly temptation. I was the one who put those little babies back together after each abortion without flinching. I should have listened to the Holy Spirit and resisted the temptation to do abortions. That baby's kick was like a wake-up-call kick to my head. It took that powerful nudge to bring me to the realization that abortions end real lives that are present, regardless of the gestational age.

Despite what you may feel about abortion and what I've said so far, let me say that I have been on the other side of this issue, leading the debate for abortion access. I changed my mind and hope to convince you to do the same. And if you agree with me, I hope to give you courage to become active in the pro-life movement. No one can stand on the sidelines and remain passive in this fight.

If you have had an abortion or been affected by one, I offer you this reassurance: the Lord Jesus Christ is rich in mercy and will forgive you no matter what you have done. Go to Him in repentance and ask Him to forgive you. John 6:37 says: "All that the Father gives me will come to me; and him who comes to me I will not cast out."

He forgave me. He will forgive you. He is waiting for you to come home.

Terry Beatley

December 1, 2009, Manhattan

The pounding of my heart seemed audible as the door slowly opened. Christine, the quiet, petite wife of Bernard N. Nathanson, M.D., welcomed me inside for the 4:00 P.M. interview with her husband, the doctor once known as America's "Abortion King." He was eighty-three years old and terminally ill. Figuratively, I was walking into the pages of history to meet the physician who deeply regretted unleashing the warped world of "women's healthcare and reproductive freedom" onto America.

Though physically frail, Dr. Nathanson's mind was sharp. "What would you like to know, Terry? I will answer anything you ask me. I have nothing to hide anymore."

His manner eased my nervousness. My questions and his answers began to flow, ranging from his miserable childhood and failed relationships to details of the National Abortion Rights Action League's nationwide plan of deception to manipulate the gullible public and decriminalize abortion.

Dr. Nathanson explained that he trained Planned Parenthood's doctors on how to perform abortions, and then

---

Terry Beatley is president of Hosea Initiative, an educational nonprofit organization, and the author of *What If We've Been Wrong? Keeping My Promise to America's "Abortion King"* (Burke, Va.: Guiding Light Books, 2016). She is leading the national endeavor to make NARAL's "Catholic strategy" widely known.

watched the organization grow to become the abortion monster it is today.

He also described his unexpected rethinking of abortion because of a scientific invention that came into widespread use in the late 1970s: "Terry, the bomb was real-time ultrasound. It made everything come alive." And the science challenged him to be "intellectually honest" with himself that abortion is murder. Period.

When he acknowledged that he had intentionally stripped the unborn child of all rights and protections, his voice was faint and raspy. I looked at his downcast eyes and felt tremendous sympathy for him. His regret was nearly tangible.

As the interview drew to a close, I felt deep compassion for this old, dying man who had become a child of God on December 8, 1996, at Saint Patrick's Cathedral. I made him an offer that would redirect my life's course for the next thirteen years.

"Dr. Nathanson, I know you are too sick to travel to get your message out, but if you have something to tell America, I promise I will carry it across our nation for you."

Pausing to contemplate, he responded carefully and deliberately in his soft, tired voice: "Yes, yes, I do. Teach them the strategy of how I deceived America, but also deliver this message: tell America that the co-founder of NARAL says to love one another. Abortion is *not* love. Stop the killing. The world needs more love. I'm all about love now."

Dr. Nathanson's eyes brightened as I shook his hand and promised him I would share his final message until it becomes common knowledge, or until *Roe v. Wade* is overturned.

The abortion industry surely hopes that the pro-life, pro-Christ conversion story of its radical founder will be sterilized with propaganda or forgotten, but God and my promise stand in the way. In fact, every time I've considered setting the goal aside, God does something to move the promise forward. In December 2019, I received an invitation to file as a friend of the court with Abby Johnson in a January 2, 2020, brief filed at the U.S. Supreme Court in *June Medical Services v. Louisiana Department of Health*. I give God the glory because now, officially recorded in the SCOTUS brief, are Dr. Nathanson's own words explaining the fiction of NARAL's claim that "abortion is a decision between a woman and her doctor." His testimony reads as follows:

> Giving [abortion] just the barest patina of a medical judgment made it infinitely more acceptable and politically more palatable. In actual fact, the abortion decision is no more the doctor's than a nose job is. It is the woman alone who decides if she wants her nose fixed, or her breasts done, or her child destroyed, and she merely involves the doctor as the instrument of her decision.[1]

Another unexpected invitation allowed me to share the story about Dr. Nathanson's redemption in September 2020 with a crowd of about a hundred thousand Christians who attended The Return, an internationally televised repentance rally on the National Mall in Washington, D.C. Then came the invitation from Dr. Robert Moynihan to draft a four-page article for the October 2020 edition of his prestigious *Inside the Vatican* magazine. That article detailed NARAL's "Catholic Strategy," which Dr. Nathanson considered "the most brilliant political strategy" of all time. The 1960s plot was implemented to intimidate Catholic bishops into silence over the abortion issue, and to manipulate Catholic voters

[1] Bernard N. Nathanson, *The Abortion Papers: Inside the Abortion Mentality* (New York: Frederick Fell Publishers, 1983), 199.

into supporting pro-abortion candidates even if they were personally against abortion!

What the abortion industry fears most is Americans uncovering what Dr. Nathanson spent his last days trying to expose:

1. The propaganda used to deceive media representatives, legislators, doctors, judges, and millions of American citizens
2. The stealth behind NARAL's "Catholic strategy"
3. The science of why breast cancer is on the rise since abortion was decriminalized
4. The fast-tracking of a racist population-control plan initiated by the founder of Planned Parenthood
5. The aggressiveness of the abortion lobby to eviscerate parental rights
6. The accuracy of Dr. Nathanson's warning to NARAL, in which he predicted that if abortion remained legal, America would experience increased violence and public turmoil, and the disintegration of the American family unit

Dr. Nathanson died on February 21, 2011. May he rest in eternal peace, and intercede, if he is able, for the restoration of respect for the unborn and the swift demise of the assembly-line slaughtering of babies in the womb.

CONCLUSION

Bernard Nathanson's story perfectly illustrates America's abortion story. Rejecting God leads to destruction on many levels, for oneself as well as others. But the story does not end in defeat. At the center of our Holy Faith is the belief that even suffering and death can be redemptive and life-giving. God can use anything, even something as evil as abortion, for His good purposes. Whether you've had an abortion, supported abortion, or performed an abortion, you are loved by a God who patiently waits to forgive you and help you write your own story of redemption. Bernard Nathanson was a secular Jew who became an abortionist and an atheist. He died a pro-life Catholic. *No one* is beyond the grasp of the merciful hands of the Father, and that means everyone has the potential to see abortion for what it is— the unjust killing of an innocent human being.

I remember a hot July morning when one woman after another was being led into Planned Parenthood by volunteer escorts. It was a surgical abortion day, which meant a two-hour clash between Planned Parenthood's people and the pro-lifers on the sidewalk. The stand-offs this day had been more contentious than usual, requiring police intervention in several altercations. As tensions were finally settling, a Providence police officer walked toward his car to leave the scene. He suddenly stopped, turned toward me, and in an exasperated voice, said, "You know, Tyler, why don't you go down to Brown University and pass out condoms or educate young people to be more responsible *before* getting pregnant? It's too late once you come down here!" I was familiar with the sentiment and considered rolling my eyes at the false assumptions built into his comment, but nevertheless, he had asked me a question, and I was going to answer it.

"You're right," I said. "The women almost never change their minds. But imagine if you were the one being led into a building to be killed. Imagine if no one showed up to defend you. We don't come here because we're going to change everyone's mind. We come here to defend the child."

"Okay. Okay, I get that," he replied. By the look on his face, it seemed like the reality of abortion hit him right between the eyes for the first time in his life. He was a man committed by his occupation to defend the weak and help serve justice in his community, yet right in the heart of his city, a child-killing factory operated with impunity.

God's truths are like seeds that are scattered across the hearts and minds of His people, waiting to be watered by the lives of the faithful.

That's what happened to a taxi driver who would often drive by that same Planned Parenthood location and see a woman named Joanne praying on her knees. One day, he stopped his cab and got out to speak to Joanne.

"Let me tell you a story," said the cab driver. "You make a difference."

The driver went on to explain to Joanne that he had seen people praying outside of the facility for a few years.

"Sometimes there's just one," he said. "I don't like that, when one of you is left alone."

A lone person praying on a sidewalk made him think.

"I asked myself why anyone would come out in the rain,

the snow, the heat, at night, in the morning—even when you're alone, and even when people are mean to you. I figured what you were doing meant something big. Why else would you do it?"

He talked about the regular prayer presence and that sign with a Bible verse that always stuck with him: "Before I formed you in the womb, I knew you" (Jer 1:5).

"What you do, praying and holding that sign, no matter what, that is enough. It speaks for itself. That's the message. But that's only the beginning of the story. When my daughter called from down south to tell me she was pregnant, I thought of you. And I never said 'abortion' to her. I just helped. Now I'm the grandfather of a two-year-old. That baby is so important, no matter what."

He then related a much more recent phone call, this time from his younger daughter.

"She has lots of difficulties and worries. Illness, financial problems, abandonment, everything. She told me she was pregnant. I thought of you people again. Again, I knew. I didn't say 'abortion.' She's seven weeks pregnant. She's going to make it. We'll work it out. We see you. It's a good thing what you do."[1]

Before I formed *you* in the womb, I knew *you*. God has a unique love for each individual, giving us our objective worth, reminding us that our lives have purpose. Abortion violates that great *you* in the prophet's words, severs the relationship between Father and child, and reduces a person's worth to a human choice. In the end, abortion is simply opposed to God's love. What did God do in His greatest

[1] Tyler Rowley's conversation with Joanne Ciocys, including e-mails that recounted the story from March 26, 2010.

act of love? He went to the Cross, showing man how to sacrifice oneself for others. Abortion teaches man how to sacrifice others for oneself.

An abortionist. A police officer. A cab driver. When the real story of abortion is told, any person can understand the brute injustice that it inflicts. There will come a day when history will judge our responses to that injustice. What did you do as sixty-three million innocent lives were ended? This book tells us the stories of what twenty-three men and women did.

What is your story?

—Tyler Rowley and Abby Johnson